YOU
VS.
WALL
STREET

YOU VS. WALL STREET

GROW WHAT YOU'VE GOT AND GET BACK WHAT YOU'VE LOST

by Natalie Pace

Vanguard Press
A Member of the Perseus Books Group

Set in 11 point Dante

Library of Congress Cataloging-in-Publication Data
Pace, Natalie.
    Put your money where your heart is : investment strategies for lifetime wealth / by Natalie Pace
        p. cm.
    ISBN 978-1-59315-491-2 (alk. paper)
    1. Stocks. 2. Investments. 3. Finance, Personal. I. Simon, William L., 1930- II. Title.
    HG4661.P33 2008
    332.63'22--dc22
                            2008021451

10 9 8 7 6 5 4 3 2 1

For Christy, Davis and Laurel
and for Arynne Simon

CONTENTS

PREFACE: AN ENTHUSIASTIC RECOMMENDATION FROM A NOBEL LAUREATE

by Dr. Gary S. Becker,
Winner of the 1992 Nobel Prize in Economics

Natalie Pace thinks of investing as "fun," and I tend to agree, as long as the amounts that people use in their trading are small enough that no great reduction in their standard of living would be required if much of the traded assets were lost. The challenge, especially to inexperienced investors, is to avoid getting carried away by some initial success into believing that you can continue to outsmart the market. Natalie offers good advice that would help to combat such excessive optimism.

Her excellent advice about how to allocate one's monthly budget with her "Buy My Own Island Plan" is an important component of achieving economic security and wealth at older ages. She also advocates considerable amounts to be set aside for basic needs, education, charities and fun things to do. This may seem obvious, but many people, including educated men and women, need help in making such basic allocations of their resources. They often get into trouble when they neglect to follow simple and fundamental rules of the type provided in this book.

I have known Natalie Pace for several years, and I have read a considerable amount of what she has written in that time. I have always found her sensible, enthusiastic and insightful. All these qualities come through in this book. This is why I recommend it with enthusiasm.

FOREWORD: BECOMING A CONSCIOUS CONDUIT OF FINANCIAL ENERGY

by Michael Bernard Beckwith,
Founder and Spiritual Director,
Agape International Spiritual Center,
Los Angeles, California

The fact that money is a sensitive subject in Western culture is often first learned in childhood. Perhaps, like me, you can recall your parents' etiquette training about not asking family members—or anyone for that matter—how much money they make or how much they paid for something. It makes you wonder how money escaped being added to the official list of "what not to discuss in polite company," along with politics, sex and religion.

Obviously, there's a lot of mental and emotional energy around the topic of money in general and one's own money in particular. Money itself is a neutral energy resource, an energy symbol of supply. Our ability to magnetize the flow of money and financial resources into our lives is beginning to be understood as a multi-dimensional activity, and Natalie Pace does an excellent service to her readers through her integral approach to investment management. Her Three-Ingredient Investment Recipe offers a success strategy that includes generous portions of knowledge, wisdom, intention-setting, integrity, confidence, courage and a spirit of generosity—qualities that are essential not only to making money, but to appreciating and multiplying it abundantly. Approaching money with these qualities—not magical thinking or other gimmicks—is the key to your becoming a conscious conduit of financial energy.

Equally important, Natalie invites her readers to consider a holistic definition of wealth, beginning with an understanding that the criteria for measuring wealth is not merely one's bank balance, but also one's state of inner happiness, health, creativity and contentment. "A life like this," she wisely points out, "increases in value every single day and becomes more valuable not just to you but to those around you as well." Money is not just about "more" for its own sake. Stabilization of our financial life-structure offers us the freedom to explore the wonders of life on our planet; to express our talents, skills and gifts; to be of service in philanthropic causes; to have time to discover the deeper meaning of our life's purpose.

A powerful metaphysical principle that Natalie emphasizes is that in order to have the energy-qualities of money work on your behalf you must first uncover your perceptions and beliefs about money and how they determine your overall relationship to your financial life. Her empowering and practical exercises for defining and shifting these beliefs impact not only how you think about money, but life itself. Natalie has synthesized practical and metaphysical techniques that will introduce you to your inner economist and thereby increase your confidence, expand your knowledge and skillfully manage your financial resources. You will find it an interesting discovery to realize how money is a mirror that reflects your relationship to many other aspects of your life.

Natalie takes the mystery and confusion out of personal finance and liberates you from the myth that Wall Street smarts are the monopoly of professional brokers. Whether your current financial means are modest or substantial, her time-tested, hands-on, interactive and intuitive methods of successful investing will assist you in dissolving your money obstacles. So prepare yourself to receive in-depth insights and practical advice that will lead you to financial wholeness. The very fact that you have purchased this book is already an investment in establishing your financial future, one that will pay rich dividends. May its humanely deep understanding be your guide to both inner and outer wealth.

PROLOGUE: GET YOUR MONEY BACK (AND NEVER LOSE IT AGAIN)

COMMON SENSE ECONOMICS:
THE WISDOM OF THE SHOPPER

I'm often asked, "Are you a Miltonian or Keynesian when it comes to Economics?"

I respond, "I'm a Dr. Seussian." I'm from the school of common-sense economics, and it has served me well through many crazy fads over the last decade, such as the "New Economy," no-doc/no-down/interest-free liar's loans, and the 2008 bailout of brokerages and banks. I can't read one squiggly line from an economic formula (truly) but let me walk the dirt of the investment, and I can sniff out the truth buried between the lines in an earnings report—and so can you.

When the earnings reports show increased earnings but the store is empty all of the time, you don't have to read the full report to know it's a lie. There is wisdom in the shopper, and as a shopper, you are getting the news months before it lands on the analyst's desk in the form of an earnings report. If you align the things you buy as a consumer with what you own as an investor, you'll get rich and enrich the world at the same time.

If you can't get to the shopping cart without the dial-up connection crashing (as happened for most Americans in 2000) and the Internet companies have been losing money for five years, NASDAQ is going to crash. When no one can afford to buy a home without fancy loan tricks, you've got prices that are unsustainable. When college students can borrow money to buy and flip homes in Florida, Arizona, Nevada, and California with a few lies on the application, housing is at the brink of the cliff.

Investor beware. In 2009, many of the banks that were reporting profits had a lot of vacant properties that they were refusing to foreclose on for over a year. And their "record earnings" were largely on overdraft fees, meaning they were sucking the life out of customers who were already on the ropes, financially. Killing your customer is not a sustainable business model.

You might be surprised that I see the average person as having so much power over the pros, but here is the truth of the matter: **Main Street owns Wall Street.** Through your IRA, 401(k), annuity and pension fund, you own the publicly traded corporations.

If you'd rather promote innovative companies and avoid the Bailout Index (that is, the leading Blue Chip Index, which had a significant number of companies that were bailed out) you would have saved your nest egg. It's as easy as *Red Fish, Blue Fish*, once you understand that you're not stuck with the four or five little boxes on the form that your Human Resources person or your Certified Financial Planner or insurance specialist hands you.

When you invest blindly, your money is too often poured into corporations that pay the highest commissions to the broker. That's how poorly run companies stay at the top of Wall Street–through cronyism economics. When you invest in the products that you love, you promote healthier companies because the ones making inferior products are challenged to attract your investment by making better products, instead of just paying a higher commission to the salesmen. They can't trick you into investing in their company or fool you with misleading press releases and earnings reports.

So does this really work? Bill and Nilo Bolden came to me in January of 2008 seeking remedy for the recession. This was before the economists were officially calling it a recession, even though Bear

Stearns had been bailed out and a number of mortgage banks had thrown in the towel. I drew a pie chart *on a napkin* (see page 92). Since their 401(k) didn't offer Exchange Traded Funds, Nilo put everything safe until she could get proper diversification. (At 55, she would have only had 25 percent in ETFs anyway). Over the next fourteen months, the Dow Jones Industrial Average lost half of its value, dropping from 13,044 at the beginning of 2008 to the low of 6547 on March 9, 2009. Bill and Nilo Bolden lost nothing.

The Boldens had plenty of friends, family and colleagues who pooh-poohed the pie chart. Hundreds of thousands of dollars were lost. One person close to the couple lost half a million dollars when she refused to heed the advice I'd given.

In fact, many people came to my investing retreats in 2008 and 2009 after their portfolios had imploded. Rita Starnes reported that her stockbroker lost over $100,000. After only a few months, Rita had already made $27,000 on her own, by investing in some clean energy stocks that she learned how to evaluate by using my Stock Report Card and 3-ingredient investment recipe. Glennda was so happy with the changes she made in her portfolio, and her returns, that she volunteered to help others at many retreats thereafter. Three other attendees formed an investment club that posted 47 percent gains between June of 2008 and June 2009!

IF YOU LOST MORE THAN 20 PERCENT, YOUR NEST EGG WAS CRACKED TO BEGIN WITH.

50 year-olds would have limited their losses to 11 percent, if they were properly diversified and had overweighted 20 percent safe at the onset of the recession. You should always keep a percent equal to your age SAFE, so the older you get, the less risk your nest egg has of getting smashed. If you were 50 and had 50 percent safe, your maximum losses were only

19 percent of your total assets (or 38 percent of only half your nest egg). If you had moved an additional 20 percent safe at the beginning of the recession–as I instructed my subscribers and Bill and Nilo Bolden to do–your maximum losses would have been only 11 percent (38 percent of only 30 percent of your portfolio). 25 year-olds who were "recession-proofed" with 45 percent safe would have limited their losses to just 21 percent (38 percent of 55 percent of their portfolio).

Why didn't your trusted financial professional planner tell you this and protect you better? The old system of buying and holding mutual funds worked for almost a century, but hasn't worked for the last decade and won't work going forward. The stock market was lower at the end of 2008 than it was in 1998, meaning that investors lost money over the last decade, if they were buying and holding mutual funds.

The financial professional in your life may know about Modern Portfolio Theory (keeping safe and diversified), but their brokerage may pay her on commission to sell you mutual funds. The system isn't set up to protect your best interests. The same goes true with financial books that talk about buy-and-hold strategies. Buying and holding mutual funds does not work in a slow growth economy, which is what the United States is in, as Baby Boomers retire.

You are not "locking in your losses" when you switch from a losing strategy to one that works. If you lost a lot of money, the crappy plan that got you there will be a poor resurrection strategy. You are where you are. The question is, "What's a better strategy going forward?"

When you see an entire industry melting down, as the insurance companies (AIG and others) and brokerages (Bear Stearns, Lehman Bros., Merrill Lynch, Smith Barney and others) have, you need to get the memo that the system is inherently flawed. Smart professionals, mostly limited to the online discount brokerages, are getting current and incorporating the strategies outlined in this book. Many investors who have followed my work for the last decade incorporated the strategies to save their nest eggs from losses in the 2000–2002 *and* the

2008 recessions, and will continue to profit, outperforming the market, going forward.

So, what is this magic system that works in bull and bear markets?

BUY AND HOLD DOESN'T WORK IN
A SLOW GROWTH ECONOMY

It's time to start resurrecting your nest egg, utilizing ETFs, Modern Portfolio Theory, annual rebalancing and common sense. This may sound complicated, but it's easy as a pie chart.

Using annual rebalancing, you would have captured 80 percent gains in NASDAQ at the beginning of 2000, and had limited exposure (less than 10% of your nest egg) to the 70 percent NASDAQ losses that occurred between 2000 and 2002. Real estate doubled between 2002 and 2007, and clean energy earned 60 cents on the dollar in 2007. That means every $100,000 becomes $180,000 during a NASDAQ boom period (such as between 1998 and 2000), or becomes $200,000 during a real estate rocket ship, or becomes $160,000 while invested in clean energy—and all of these gains occurred in a single year! There are big gains to be made in this brave, new world.

Just as you can't heal high blood pressure with the same old doughnuts, coffee and couch-potato plan, you are not going to get a better bottom line by sitting around, doing nothing and praying that things get better. You are the architect of your life. The Certified Financial Planner is the contractor who should be assisting you in building your dream-come-true living and providing you with the best options for tax-protected accounts for your stocks, like IRAs, 401(k)s, health savings accounts, college savings accounts and more.

Start with reading this book. If you want to create a plan immediately that will work for the rest of your life, register for one of my Get Rich and Enrich Retreats. Go to NataliePace.com for details.

And remember, when Wall Street acts like the town drunk, they are driving your car with your gas. So, if you want to send Wall Street to rehab, it's time to lay down a new set of rules of how the Street behaves with your hard-earned dollars. Curfew your investments in the status quo. Blind faith in Wall Street was as silly as giving the car keys to your teenager on prom night.

Every cent you own and every moment you spend is always an investment. So, live within your dreams. Create the means. And know that your common sense and conscious ownership in corporate America is the best investment you'll ever make–for your own success as well as the betterment of our world. Wall Street can't package and sell nonsense, like the subprime loans, if consumers aren't there to buy them.

So have a little faith (not blind faith) that you can do this, if you just get the right tools and education. You'll find out how to make the magic of Stock Report Cards and pie charts work to provide you with money while you sleep in the pages that follow.

MAKE LOVE WITH YOUR MONEY

Idi Amin died in exile. King Richard III died for lack of a horse. Kenneth Lay wasn't the only multimillionaire to die broke. On the other hand, Gandhi, Mozart, Queen Elizabeth I, Mother Teresa and Dr. Martin Luther King Jr. continue to live richly in memory all the days of humanity. During their lives they enjoyed the delight and satisfaction of living each day in pursuit of their life's purpose. Rich, powerful tyrants who love money more than anything else end up surrounded by sycophants and body snatchers, while Gandhi, Simone Weil, Mother Teresa and the others listed above had all their needs met and were fueled from the inside out by fulfilling a powerful life mission every day.

There is a clear, underreported trend here. Jerks end up broke. Really big jerks end up broke and exiled or dead, which is a poor way to plod through life. Creative people who work hard to make our world a more beautiful place are supported and have a lot of others invested in making sure their basic needs are met. Who is really rich here: the villains or the saints of our collective evolution?

You are a creator of our world. Your retirement dollars are invested in the corporations that define our existence. When you realize the power of your money and investments as tools to make you rich and to also enrich our world, you will start aligning yourself with other creative and motivated people who are invested in your success, the success of the companies you choose to support with your investment dollars and the world at large.

That is why I use such a provocative title for this foreword—*Make Love with Your Money*. I am touching pleasure points in your brain when I talk about money intentionally—to spark your endorphins. Most people still believe the old myths about money, and they carry around a lot of anger, worry, doubt, fear and loathing about wealth. "Why is that person rich? I'd make a much better rich person! I'm the one who *deserves* to be rich. Why wasn't I born as lucky as her?"

BEING THE CEO OF YOUR OWN SUCCESS

What does any of this have to do with trading stocks? Once you come to understand that you are, right now, the creator of your world—your home, your neighborhood and by the money you invest in your retirement plan, even the world at large—you will start thinking like a rich person instead of a victim. Victims fear money, worry about money, think that they are owed money, think they deserve money more than the next guy, and spend all their time gambling or trying to win the lottery, instead of embracing healthy money habits that lead to lasting wealth.

Too many people have fear around money. I call it "investing with stomach acid" instead of your intellect. When you trade with fear, the odds are that you will buy high and sell low. That is what fear does, even though it is the exact opposite thing that everyone knows with their brain to do.

Believing you have to make money fast before the world ends or the bank takes back your home is the kind of vulnerability that scam artists and shysters feed upon. When you secretly believe that you are going to lose money on your investments, you don't drink in the education and research you need in order to make a successful purchase in the first place. When you make wise, informed investments in companies that you believe are creating the best products and services on the planet, then you believe that you are going to make a fortune in the markets, not that you are going to lose. When you invest in what you know and love, your wisdom as a shopper and your passion about the product will immobilize fear, and that's when you can really start making confident and correct choices that will pay off for you. You know how to place a value on what you own and are less likely to sell it on the cheap. Imagine now how it would feel to own Google at the Initial Public Offering (IPO). Or Microsoft. Or Suntech Power Holdings (a solar energy manufacturer). Or Starbucks. Or Toyota.

BECOME THE BEST YOU

Some authors make investing too complicated. Others make it too boring. Some have cookie-cutter investment strategies, like cutting out coffee or using fancy software, that frankly don't work because no two people have the same talents, passions, goals, time or intelligence. I am asking you to think about the power of your money to transform and enrich your own life and the world at large and to apply my strategies to become the best *you*. My investment recipe works because *you* supply the ingredients. The Billionaire Game works because *you* decide what's charity, what's education, what's fun and what to invest in, and the fact that *you* are *invested* in achieving your own success—instead of relying on someone else to do it or drowning in basic needs—is the fuel that drives prosperity.

CHOOSING FAITH OVER FEAR

It's not that hard to switch your thinking from fear that you're going to lose everything to faith that you can become wise and rich. It's not more time spent. If you think of all the time you spend worrying about money, you know that getting smart about investing is actually going to take *less time*. Becoming a successful investor who earns gains while you sleep costs less than being a fear-based investor who loses money every time the economy hits a recession. It's simply investing the same money you put in your 401(k) or IRA more effectively.

If you can shop, you can pick stocks. If you tithe, you can become a millionaire. If you can pick a great life partner, then you can select the second most important person in your life: your certified financial planner. If you know your age, then you know what percent of your retirement plan you should keep safe, i.e. *not* invested in stocks. Once you discover how the dollars you invest create our world, you can start investing in the products, goods and services that will make our planet a great place to live.

How would you live if you had all the money in the world? What companies would you invest in? The beauty of the stock market is that with very little money, you can create that life now. You can become not just a rich person and a great investor, but someone who does all that by putting her money where her heart is—by making love with money. When people start investing with heart and soul and wisdom, instead of fear, blind faith and greed, this world will become a very, very beautiful place. There is no end to the problems that can be solved when we move trillions out of the old industries of oil, gas and cigarettes and invest it in clean energy, goods and services that contribute to a healthy, sustainable world.

MAKE LOVE WITH YOUR MONEY

That is how I went from a Copper Miner's Daughter to Wall Street Golden Girl; it's how I went from Divorced and Desperate to my dream-come-true life. When you start investing in things that you know and love, instead of with fear and greed, your life will change immediately, and this world will become a much more beautiful place. A life like this increases in value every single day and becomes more valuable not just to you but to those around you as well.

PART 1

Get Educated

1

FROM COPPER MINER'S DAUGHTER TO WALL STREET GOLDEN GIRL

You have to trust in something—your gut, destiny, life, karma, whatever—because believing that the dots will connect down the road will give you the confidence to follow your heart, even when it leads you off the well-worn path.
—Steve Jobs, CEO and cofounder of Apple,
former CEO and cofounder of Pixar Animation

Divorce sucks. Your fairy tale is shattered. Your expenses double. You're wracked with guilt. You're afraid that only creeps get divorced. (That's your new dating pool, plus, you're now one of the creeps.) To make the situation worse, you probably can't afford your home anymore.

It might surprise you to learn that almost 40 percent of married couples will end up divorced within ten years and the average age of widowhood is fifty-seven.

When a life crisis comes at you—and it will—you will feel so overwhelmed with responsibility, fatigue, hopelessness, time constraints and grief that the temptation to trust in strangers on serious and consequential matters will feel like a matter of necessity. In fact, that is

---

* I originally wrote this chapter at the request of Christine Kloser, and it appears in her 2004 book, *From Inspiration to Realization*.

the time to trust your instincts most. That doesn't mean all of your choices will pan out perfectly, but you will be on the right path.

When I got hit with the sledgehammer of divorce and the challenges of providing a home for my son, I thought, "Teaching. I'll be home for my kid after school, and I'll make decent money." How naïve I was. When you consider teachers don't get paid to be at school early, or to stay late or to grade papers into the middle of the night, my housekeeper was earning more per hour than I was.

Within two years of teaching, I was so far behind on my bills that the county was threatening to put a lien on my one asset—my condominium—to collect the property taxes I owed. My credit card debt had blossomed into a nuclear waste dump that I stored on the top of my refrigerator—so toxic that it made your eyes bleed just to pass by. Needless to say, I was an emotional wreck, and I could only approach the nuclear fallout of which bills to pay, which companies to plead with and which to completely ignore on the nights when my son went to his father's. How could I have let things get to this point? What kind of world expected me to work all day just to provide basic necessities and then criticized me for having a latchkey kid who turned to drugs or video games for comfort?

Complaining doesn't pay the bills. I stopped and looked at my degree hanging on the wall and made myself a commitment. It was just a bachelor's degree in English Literature (though summa cum laude—that should count for something). I would find a way to parlay it into a better-paying position.

And I did. I landed an executive-level position at a nationwide phone company. It was a small office owned by a friend of mine. Initially, the position was on a trial basis, but within a few months, under my operational direction, the company was out of the red and into the black and my position became more secure. The salary was double what I earned as a teacher, and the hours, though longer on paper, were much less in reality.

At the same time, the wonder of investment cycles began to work in my favor. In 1998, at the time of my divorce, I was locked into a home that I couldn't afford and couldn't sell. It was only a two bedroom, so I couldn't even rent out a room to help make up the difference.

Real estate had been depressed for most of the 1990s, and my mortgage was underwater due to a series of Los Angeles disasters—the Rodney King riots, fires in Malibu, mudslides and an earthquake in Northridge. We were waiting for the locusts to come. Things were so dire that in 1994 you could have bought a home north of Montana Avenue in Santa Monica for $750,000. (In 2006, you couldn't buy a termite-ridden hut there for under $2 million.) By spring 2000, however, the Los Angeles real estate market came roaring back. I borrowed money, gave my crappy little condo a new coat of paint and carpets and sold it for a small profit.

Burned for nine years by my first major real estate investment, I turned my eye to Wall Street. You could have thrown a dart at a wall full of stocks and found a winner in 1999, and cocktail parties were abuzz with people touting their gains. When stocks began dipping in 2000, many people considered it a buying opportunity.

On a breezy Santa Monica lunch period, I met with a certified financial planner recommended to me by my banker. Steven Snappy (obviously not his real name, which I've forgotten) had been referred by my bank and had a set of impressive initials after his name—NASD, SIPC and so on, which lent him credibility. I sat down, feeling as though I was in good hands. He served up a pie chart telling me that if I tossed my real estate profits into a bowl of mutual funds, I'd churn up a minimum of 12 to 15 percent return. If, that is, I also dumped in an additional $500 a month, which was the minimum amount I could commit to.

"Twelve to 15 percent," he said in a whisper, behind a cupped hand, "is very conservative." (Never mind the fact that I'd have to give up eating to afford $500 per month.) His mutual fund brochures, which I still have, boasted up to 43 percent returns on funds anchored by AOL, Global Crossing and Enron, to name three. These brochures quoted returns from March 2000, at the stock market high, something Mr. Snappy neglected to tell me, even though our meeting occurred in September 2000 after NASDAQ had already tumbled about 40 percent.

When I met Snappy, I thought "P/E" was the company in the movie about Erin Brokovich. I had no idea what Cisco did. I did know, however, that the telecommunications companies were overbooking revenue. As an executive in that industry, I was on the phone daily trying to get hundreds of thousands of dollars worth of credits from a major company that had been over-billing my company at triple the contracted rate for almost a year. If telecommunications companies were cooking the books, what other companies were doing it?

Snappy became very impatient with my questions. It was perfectly easy to see from his charts that the mutual funds he was recommending were amazing, he insisted. By diversifying, I would be protected from the fluctuations of any one sector. How hard was it to see this. Besides, he was making a huge, unauthorized exception for me by lowering the minimum buy-in. If my money sat in savings at 4 to 5 percent interest, that was less than inflation. We were talking *ten* times gains in upside potential. Just what was it I didn't understand? (If you ever hear someone talking to you like this, remember s/he is a *salesperson*, not an investment genius, and you should *run*.)

There I was—a professional woman in sharp new clothes with a pen poised to sign a slew of documents I didn't believe in because I wanted some sleazy salesperson to approve of me. *Think fast, Natalie.*

At the time, Al Gore was campaigning on eight years of prosperity and how he was going to be the candidate to continue it. It didn't matter whether Gore or Bush was elected; over 50 percent of the nation wasn't going to be happy about it. In fact, who could continue eight years of prosperity? And didn't it take a few years for the rookie in office to figure out how to get anything done? How could technology companies like Amazon.com continue to operate for *years* in the red? So many red flags. Too many.

I left that day without signing, using the lame excuse that I was late for work. Snappy was exasperated with me but that didn't keep him from continually calling and nagging me to sign the documents. I was too busy researching P/Es, PEGs, Debt/Equity ratios and the 10-Ks of my favorite companies to spend time offering him more ridiculous excuses. (Thank God for the ignore option on my cell phone!)

By the end of 2000, while I still only understood the basics of all of this new terminology, I had a very good idea that the markets were continuing to drop and that the recession was deepening—in other words, my instincts that the companies were overpriced was proving to be accurate. So instead of throwing away my life savings on Snappy's "big winners" (Enron, Global Crossing and AOL), my investment chugged along at 5 percent interest in a certificate of deposit.

What was the top-performing asset class of the year 2000?

Cash.

When I did invest in the stock market in August of 2001, when Opsware was on sale at 83 percent off, I tripled my money in just four short months—without shorting. I walked into the brokerage dancing on the ceiling at the end of December 2001. I can remember only a handful of times being that elated over money—when I bought my first car, when I purchased my first home, and when I tripled my money in the stock market. I did feel a little sorry for the others in the brokerage who were cashing out of their holdings to cover losses. Some were cashing out to cover their living expenses. The broker had a hard time believing that I was in there to capture my gains!

Since then, I've had extraordinary gains in the markets. And I was able to found and become the majority shareholder in my own financial news company, all of which led to this book.

THE BOTTOM LINE

I'm thrilled I didn't lose all of my money with Steven Snappy, but the most important gain I received that year was confidence. When you have nagging doubts, remember: it's your heart begging for more information. Trust that your uneasy spirit knows something. By prospecting into the heart and soul of your concerns and educating yourself to answer those concerns intelligently, you will start on your path to financial wisdom. Knowledge and information are better strategies for decision-making than blind trust in a stockbroker—or anyone for that matter.

This book will give you the tools you need to sharpen your own intellect. And the great thing is that it is not about mind-numbing charts or getting a Ph.D. in economics. Rather than trying to teach you how to think like a Wall Street analyst, I'm going to teach you how to use and value information that you already have as a consumer and an employee. And the great news about using your skills as a shopper as a strategy for successful investing is that you get your information three months or more before it shows up on an analyst's desk. You are also investing in the products, goods and services that you most love—a win for you as a shopper, as an investor and for the company's continued health.

NATALIE'S THREE TAKEAWAY TIPS

1. Your instincts and questions are a call to learn more. Trust them.
2. If you can't afford your home, it's time to get a better-paying job, a roommate or both.
3. Brokers and lovers: it pays to pick a good one!

THE THREE-INGREDIENT RECIPE FOR COOKING UP PROFITS

If you like the store, chances are you'll love the stock.
—PETER LYNCH

I got into this business because a large number of my friends came crying to me at the end of 2001, saying that their husbands or their brokers had lost half or more of their stock portfolio and begging me to "teach them what I know." They were quite a bit more humble than they had been just a few years earlier. At Christmas parties in 1999, I'd told everyone within hearing range to sell their NASDAQ. I didn't have extreme confidence then, as I do now, that I was a great stock picker. I just knew that if you had made 900 percent gains, the only way to ensure you kept them was to lock them in by selling. I also knew that when companies lose money for five years, something wasn't adding up. Money doesn't grow on trees after all. Sooner or later the people doling out loans and investment capital were going to stop doing so, and when that happened, if the company was still in the red, it would bleed out and go bankrupt. I also understood that it was going to be impossible to have the world shopping online if everyone's dial-up connection was as crappy as mine was.

Most of my friends just avoided me and my wet blanket concerns so they could go on bragging about the 900 percent they'd made on AOL. Who wanted to talk to a killjoy who was so stupid as to think they had to sell their stocks *now* and pay taxes on the capital gains? I was just a silly little single mom who lived in a condo. (Even though I had become vice president at a telecommunications company, most still thought of me as a part-time schoolteacher who had no clue of the tax considerations of rich people.) The few people who did stop to talk to me only did so to tell me how stupid I was for not understanding the "New Economy."

While I would have rather taught my friends what I knew *before* they lost all of their money, I was happy to enlighten them in 2001 so that they might prevent those kinds of losses from ever happening again. Since these were upper-middle-class soccer moms with to-do lists a mile long, I wanted to make investing as much fun as shopping. (Incidentally, these women, who were much richer than I was, came to be my friends from the nonprofit organizations that I donated my time to. More on that later.)

I wanted to give them a strategy that worked as reliably as a recipe. And I wanted investing to be something they could do once or twice a month, if they loved trading, or once or twice a year, if they wanted to take a long-term approach. I don't obsessively watch television or pray that the stock price will go up more than down every day, so I wanted to assure them that these principles were sound and could hold up against another recession.

I believe (and so do Peter Lynch and Warren Buffett) that the average investor can do great in the stock market simply by sticking with companies they know something about. Buying stocks at random, without having a strong sense of or passion for a product, means you could risk buying high or at the sunset of a product's popularity (a money-losing proposition). There are lots of gurus out there (with mixed credibility) who offer all kinds of tips and expensive software to evaluate investments. I offer, instead, a simple, easy-to-use, easy-to-understand recipe that allows you to size up the company you know and love—by lining it up against the competition—and evaluate the price so that you never pay retail for the stock.

Learning the formula takes as long as it takes to read this book. Applying the formula takes less time than most people are already spending mainlining the daily, largely superfluous and confusing "news" on every company traded on Wall Street. Completing a Stock Report Card™ on the company you're interested in and two competitors should take about twenty minutes, less time if you employ power searches to get the information. That's the beauty of wisdom. Same amount of time and money = better results.

My Three-Ingredient Investment Recipe for cooking up profits is the foundation of *all* successful investing, whether it is stocks, bonds,

---

NATALIE'S NOTE

There is one key consideration to the Three-Ingredient Investment Recipe for successful investing in individual stocks and investments: You should not be trading your nest egg or your house, condo or apartment to do it. That would be like juggling eggs, too risky that you'll break a few. When setting up and/or reviewing your retirement plan and the home that you live in, be sure you:

- have your money properly allocated across assets (bonds, money markets, stocks, etc.).
- have a long-term plan.
- employ a rational roadmap to get there.
- make sure that you will enjoy your investments (so you can sleep at night).
- keep enough cash on hand.
- protect a percentage equal to your age by investing that portion in bonds, treasury bills, certificates of deposits or money markets.
- employ an experienced, ethical and talented Certified Financial Planner.
- maximize as many of the tax-free strategies as possible!

---

real estate, classic cars, postage stamps or even Beanie Babies. When your evaluation strategy starts getting too complicated or the statistics make your head swim, make sure that your desired investment passes the muster of this recipe. Keep it handy. Be religious about adhering to it. It works—every time.

We'll discuss nest-egg strategies later on in the book. For now, we're going to focus on earning great gains in individual stocks (a smaller portion of your retirement plan) by starting with your heart, seasoning with the wisdom you already have as a shopper and adding a little brainpower to the mix.

NATALIE'S THREE-INGREDIENT INVESTMENT
RECIPE FOR COOKING UP PROFITS
1. Start with what you know and love.
2. Pick the leader in the sector (in real estate, it's location, location, location).
3. Buy low; sell high (easy to say; hard to do).

Any time a potential investment seems too complicated and twists your mind into endless debates, go back to the simplicity of this formula. If it doesn't pass this test, just say, "Not now." You still need more information before you can make a well-informed decision.

Be disciplined about following the recipe. You need all of the ingredients, and if you take the steps out of order, you could end up with a brick that sinks your profits rather than a cake that rises light and fluffy to Cloud 9. Since we all want to vacation on Cloud 9 before we're ninety, let's sharpen your skills and start cooking.

Step One: Start With What You Know and Love
The first ingredient is easy enough. If you want to invest in infrastructure in India, and you've never been there, you have to commit to visiting India and doing a lot of research or be disciplined enough to just say no to the investment.

Warren Buffett, one of the most successful investors of all time, is notorious for *not* investing in NASDAQ. He didn't understand or care about technology enough to compete with his buddy Bill Gates (and conversely, Bill Gates is heavy in technology and lighter in insurance— one of Buffett's fields of expertise). In the latter part of the 1990s, Warren was ridiculed for missing out on the rocket ship gains that the NASDAQ enjoyed. He missed the high *and* he missed the crash landing, and meanwhile, his returns chugged along for steady, reliable, strong gains.

What few people realize is that trading individual stocks is a tennis match. One person wins (buys low; sells high) and the other loses (buys high; sells low). A novice is a sitting pigeon for the master. Imagine stepping out on the tennis court with Roger Federer (who by the fall of 2008 had already won thirteen Grand Slam tennis titles) and expect to even see a ball coming at you. Very unlikely.

If you don't know the first thing about a company or its product and you're not excited enough to get savvy, why step on the court and humiliate yourself with a devastating loss to the pros? Instead, focus on long-term results and proper nest-egg diversification strategies, find the perfect broker (who is your second most important life partner), and tithe to the plan from every paycheck. The average returns of the stock market over the last twenty-five years have been over 11 percent (higher than real estate), so that discipline alone could make you a millionaire.

Over the years, I've come across a lot of people who say that they don't know anything about anything, which is completely untrue. My police officer cousin found Taser International, my 2003 Company of the Year, which went on to earn up to 9,000 percent gains over the next three years. Whatever you do for a living gives you an insider's view of something. Your cleaning lady or people on the janitorial crew where you work know why they like certain cleaning products over others. I use a carpet cleaner who has taken the trouble to become the expert on organic cleaning products. You have some passion and some expertise. I'm simply giving you a framework within which to use it.

Of course, just loving the product or the store doesn't prove the stock is a good deal or that the company will continue to beat out the competition. That's why there are two other steps.

Step Two: Pick the Leader in the Sector

The second ingredient is easy to come by when you line up the numbers in my Stock Report Card (see Chapter 6) and ask the Four Basic Questions for Picking Winning Stocks (Chapter 5).

For those of you who really have a taste for investing in individual stocks—and who hasn't wanted to invest in some product that s/he loves!—picking the leader in a sector is not overly complicated. Picking the leader means that you have to take a devil's advocate approach to the product that you know and love. There were people who were buying an interest in the leading maker of horse-drawn carriages just when Ford was releasing its first motor car. People were buying stock in Worldcom the year before Skype began giving away free long distance over the Internet. You have to determine whether or not the product, company or real estate will be valuable to buyers *in the future*.

Every month, I go through the exact same research and analysis on a different sector, employ this exact recipe, ask my four questions and inevitably there's one company that's leading the pack. And that company is usually pretty easy to identify because it shines in more than one category. Better yet: none of these strategies require earning a Ph.D. in economics or sitting at your computer watching the markets every day at the crack of dawn.

Interview your friends and neighbors on whether or not they like the product or service or prefer the competition. (Don't ask your friends about the stock; ask them about the product. It's their preferences as consumers/users of the good that you want to know, not their layman's opinion on Wall Street strategies.) Ask them the four questions if you really want to get them to deeply consider their love of the product.

Remember: the CEO is the soul of the company. Get to know the CEO of the company you love and the competition a little better by researching some of her speeches online and/or reading the CEO's Note to Shareholders in the company's annual report. (The annual reports should be available on the SEC.gov web site, as well as the company's web site.)

Once you pick the leader in a sector, the final determination is simply whether or not you're buying for a good price or paying through the nose.

Step Three: Buy Low, Sell High

The third ingredient in the recipe is largely a game of mastering your emotions as much as employing strategies for identifying the low and high prices.

Buying low and selling high is completely against human nature. Buying low means that when everyone is crying Apocalypse, you're seeing Opportunity. Selling high means that you're leaving the party at midnight (sober), while all the punch drunks are screaming that the party is going till dawn, and you're going to "Miss out, man. If you just hang out a little while longer, imagine how much more fun you'll have."

No one has a crystal ball on when the low and high of an investment will occur, but there are a number of factors you need to consider before you make a buying or selling decision.

CALENDAR TRENDS
- Santa Rally
- Back-to-School Stock Sales
- Summer Doldrums
- Preelection Year Rally

OTHER CONSIDERATIONS
- Natural Disasters
- Small Caps for Performance
- Large Caps for Stability
- Exchange Traded Funds versus Mutual Funds
- Diversification and Asset Allocation
- Happy People Make Better Products Faster and Cheaper
- The Economics of Freedom
- Emerging Markets

HISTORICAL PERFORMANCE

If you already have some market experience, you might be stunned to notice that I haven't included P/E—price-to-earnings ratio—on this list. Yes, price-to-earnings ratio counts, but the above factors can be as important to determining the optimum buy/sell time as P/E is. When you read the P/E discussion later in these pages, you'll start understanding why.

If you don't know price-to-earnings ratio from hieroglyphics, don't worry. It's not difficult to understand "Never Pay Retail" and "Buy Low, Sell High." It's pretty easy to find out what the 52-week high and low prices are or even what the five-and ten-year highs and lows are, to use as a gauge. Start now with what you understand and accept that you will continue to gain knowledge as you keep reading.

Mastering The Three-Part Recipe—Water Your Money Tree: Your Brain
Write out the Three-Ingredient Recipe on an index card and stick it up in your office—or wherever you do your investments—until thinking about investing this way becomes second nature. This recipe works every time—except in an apocalypse . . . and if one of those comes, you'll have much bigger problems to worry about.

THE BOTTOM LINE

You already have the tools you need to become successful in investing. The reason you might have lost money in the past is that you didn't trust your wisdom (you placed blind faith in someone else's), or you didn't tithe regularly, or you didn't have a disciplined approach to profit-taking (like the recipe offers), or you didn't ask enough questions before jumping in (like the four questions force you to do), or you didn't have the fundamentals of a diversified, asset allocation plan in place that changes as you age.

Investments are like a mosaic. The more tiles you uncover, the clearer the picture. If you plunge your head in the sand and rely solely on the plan of a broker you hardly know, or on a single hot tip, or any other *single* piece of the puzzle, don't be surprised if your nest egg lies broken in pieces, never quite assembled into the life of your dreams.

Following the ups and downs of a stock price is not educating yourself. It's obsessing and may lead to an ulcer or, worse, a heart attack. Do your research and evaluation *before* you buy, and you'll be able to sleep soundly when the markets are unruly. Many investments treat you to a jittery period of volatility before they go on to great gains. Successful investors almost always go through a price roller-coaster before the stock soars. The roller-coaster ride can be totally worth it in the end, if you're not having a heart attack. (If you have confidence that your investment is a winner, the ups and downs of the market will seem more like a child having a temper tantrum than *Apocalypse Now*.)

If your potential investment passes all three criteria of the investment recipe, odds are in your favor to start getting rich the easy way— by following your heart and adding your brain.

NATALIE'S THREE TAKEAWAY TIPS

1. The path to investing wisdom is like learning a foreign language. The words sound like gobbledygook in the beginning, but as you keep talking, you start understanding more and more words, and soon enough you can master the language. There's no shortcut. Just start talking.
2. Investments are like a mosaic. The more tiles you turn over, the clearer picture you'll have of the health of the investment.
3. Picking the leader in the sector is the most difficult task. It pays to fill out a Stock Report Card and ask the four basic questions, which are outlined in Chapters 5 and 6.

3

PUT YOUR MONEY WHERE YOUR HEART IS

Be the change you wish to see.
—MAHATMA GANDHI

The fundamental difference between this book and other personal finance books is my premise that successful investing begins with investing in what you love. When you invest in what you love, you know the value of what you own, and you'll be less tempted to sell it off cheap. That gives you a big advantage on Wall Street. Most people don't have a clue what they own and are just nabbing and dumping on hysteria, or headline news or some crystal-ball reading strategy or software program that will fail them big time at some juncture.

I developed a holistic view of wealth (that pleasure and passion are priceless) early on in life—probably because I'm the youngest of four children. My older brother and two older sisters wore out my parents, so that by the time I came along—an accident, five years after the other three—I was ignored a lot of the time. I didn't think I was abandoned; I thought I was free.

We only had enough money for each of us to have one pair of shoes for the year, so all summer we went without shoes and bought the new pair right before school started. I had no clue that the reason I had no shoes those summer months was because we couldn't afford them. I loved going barefoot in the summer because in the sweltering Arizona sun, the tar on the road melted between your toes, and it felt great to me. I never missed not having shoes in the summertime, and actually felt that my life was *enriched* by going barefoot.

My father was a copper miner and worked as a welder in the smelter. He came home every day covered in an inch of soot. One year, for well over six months, the company workers were on strike, and our family lived on a staple diet of beans. Since I love beans and didn't really like the taste of meat, I felt like I was being spoiled, instead of deprived, by getting to eat beans every day and not being forced to eat meat every night at dinner.

Even though my family was very, very poor, I always felt very, very spoiled and indulged—doing all of the things that I most loved. My primary motivation in life has always been to enjoy it—that's what makes me feel rich—and it turns out that is the best bargaining position at all negotiating tables, even Wall Street. You have to care about what you own enough that you'll say no when someone offers you a bad price. You have to hold out for what you know is the right exchange value. You have to realize that you are not just trading for dollars—you are trading ownership in real companies, run by real people with real products that enrich (or degrade) our world.

When I set out to teach my friends what I knew about investing in the stock market, I didn't do it to become rich or famous. I did it because I loved making complicated concepts easy to understand. I also liked the idea of helping the average person become more empowered. And finally, yes, I do believe that our world will become a much more beautiful place when the average individual can check off Exchange Traded Funds of clean energy and DNA-based cancer cures instead of oil and cigarettes in their 401(k). Imagine how fast we'd stop our dependence upon oil if a trillion dollars were invested in finding the cleanest, most efficient wind, solar and geothermal power to supercharge our electric cars and railways!

In fact, if I were working on a trading desk making rich people richer, I probably would not have become the number one stock picker. Becoming the number one stock picker required a lot of long days. Since I was doing what I loved, many times I fell asleep researching stocks, whereas if I were just working a job I didn't care about, I probably would have done something else after dinner. If I were just staying up late to afford another pair of designer shoes, I doubt that I would have been so passionate about my research, analysis, stock picking and writing. (Remember: I'm the woman who really likes going barefoot.) And that's going to be true with you, too. When you find your passion and put your money there, you're going to make a lot more money for a thousand reasons; you have all of your internal pistons firing at the same target.

If you're investing in companies you care about, you're going to have your antenna up for news on them. You're going to go out of your way to test the product or visit the store. You'll ask the customer service representative on the phone about upcoming product launches or what it's like to work at the company. You'll be turning over more pieces to the puzzle than if you buy XYZ widget-maker based in Taiwan with a web site of Chinese characters. All of this is important for determining the low entry price and the beautiful high selling price. In other words, *investing in what you love allows you to harness your natural mood fluctuations in service of a higher intelligence.*

When you stick to what you know and love, it's soooo much easier to make money. You know which T-shirts wash and wear better; which olive oil has a more delightful flavor; which car has the best turning radius; which bank looks after its clients and which one seduces them in with teaser rates that jump to usury rates in six months; which major coffee retailer has the most delicious and nutritious baked goods, salads, snacks and so forth. Good quality products sold for a reasonable price tend to have a longer shelf life.

And here is where women—the shoppers of the world—really have a power that has been underutilized by Wall Street (and Main Street). Women make most of the buying decisions in the home—from where the family goes on vacation, to what the family eats, to clothes, to interior decorating and much more. Investing in the products you use every day, the ones you feel most passionate about, makes perfect sense. So if husbands and wives started comparing their shopping lists to the investing list, that alone could improve the gains enjoyed by the family.

If you invest in what *you* know and love, your odds of making money are *much* higher. When you're dealing with complicated things that you don't understand and don't believe in or when you're buying and selling on another person's advice, you have no way of gauging whether or not you're buying low and selling high.

Years ago, a friend I'll call Alice came to me after she had invested in uranium. Actually, she *thought* she had invested in uranium, but what she had actually invested in was a financial services company that invests in uranium and other products. This company was trading off the boards. (Translation: a very high-risk investment.) The share price fell from $12 to $5, and she basically just wanted to sell the stock because she was disheartened, didn't know enough about the company to know whether the share price would come back, worried that it would continue to drop, and had no way of gauging what to do—other than relying upon the advice of the person who had said that she was assured of making a killing with the investment. (That person may actually have been paid to sell her the security.)

I asked Alice what motivated her to choose the stock in the first place, as she clearly had no idea exactly what she had invested in. "My mentor told me I could triple my investment quickly, so I jumped on it," she told me.

"Who is this mentor?" I asked.

It turns out that her mentor was someone she had never met. Alice had signed up for a conference with an author she liked, then bought the mentor program from a speaker at that author's conference. She couldn't even remember the *name* of her mentor and had never asked for that person's experience, credentials, track record or even the companies that s/he'd worked for! In fact, the only reason Alice was listening to her mentor was because she had paid so much for the mentoring program that she wanted to get her money's worth—even if it meant losing thousands of dollars on the investments the mentor recommended!

When it's *all about money*, it's natural to panic when your investment doesn't start making the money you were promised and instead starts sucking the life out of your nest egg. You want to kill the disease quickly just to stop the pain and let yourself sleep at night, even if it means selling for a loss. Hmmm, so you're going to spend a fortune on strangers/mentors, questionable, high-risk investments, antianxiety medication and blood pressure pills, while your emotions soar and tumble on the *idea* of money—when you could be enjoying your life and improving your life*style* by investing in the products, goods and services that you actually use!

When I explained all of this to Alice, and then showed her how to start applying passion (love of the company and its products) instead of greed (love of money) for financial gain, she started to feel better right away.

PANICKING *NEVER* PAYS

The tendency to buy high on hot tips and sell low on headlines and hysteria is rampant. This is one of the most common investing mistakes—relying on the advice of others and thinking that they know a lot more than you do. A lot of people have tried to tell me to do a lot of things with my money over the years, and not one of them, even the so-called professionals, would have come close to making me the amount of money that I've made myself by investing in what I love—even before I became good at this. Most of the advice I've received, and I know a lot of very smart people, would have cost me an arm and a leg, and those are pounds of flesh that I want to keep.

You'll have more patience for price fluctuation if you believe in the product or service and in the company and understand why the price might be under attack in the short-term by the uninformed but remains a good investment for the wise. You'll have more confidence in your decision-making, which means that you will not whimsically base your decisions on fear and change your mind on every new headline. You might even become an activist investor, meaning that you'll provide input to the company on new products/services and/or direction that you'd like to see.

Let's say that your favorite clothing company found out that one of their production shops in Asia was busted for hiring children. You might be more inclined to find out if that was a rogue subcontractor or a common practice and buy more of the stock when it sinks, instead of just dumping the stock on bad news. If you stick with a great company during a hard time by buying *instead of* selling, you will be the visionary, the winning investor in that scenario. That is a classic case of buying low: when no one else believes in the underlying quality that you know exists.

In September 1982, Johnson & Johnson's stock was hit with the Tylenol cyanide tragedy. Someone spiked Tylenol with cyanide. Seven people in the Chicago area died, and the market share of Tylenol sank like a rock, dropping almost overnight from 35 percent to nothing. Johnson & Johnson's share price imploded, down 30 percent at a time when the stock market was having a rally. Today, that drop would have been far more dramatic because more people own individual stocks and can trade at a moment's notice with two clicks of a mouse. At the time, getting rid of stocks in a mutual fund was far more time-consuming, expensive and bothersome.

Both Tylenol sales and the Johnson & Johnson stock price rebounded in a hurry, however. Two months after the hit—talk about fast problem-solving—Tylenol capsules were reintroduced in a new, triple-sealed package. Johnson & Johnson stock rallied back that same month and was up 10 percent by January 1983. Within a few years, Tylenol was back to being the most popular over-the-counter analgesic in the United States. Today Johnson & Johnson (JNJ) is worth 2,500 percent more than it was before this crisis.

Anyone who panicked and sold on the horrible news of that fall 1982 really popped their own portfolio, as many people do when a company is the target of hysterical headlines. It took a lot of calm assurance for investors to know that Johnson & Johnson and Tylenol would survive the scrutiny and come up with a quick solution to the tampering problem—which they were able to do before the bad press and jokes about "killing headaches" could become so synonymous with their brand that they would never have been able to recover.

Johnson & Johnson is now widely admired for their handling of that event, for the quick disclosure of the problem to their customers, and for the rapid solutions they employed to prevent the murderer from having further access to continue the killing. (For the record, the killer was believed to have put the poison in at the point of retail, not manufacturing or wholesale. The person was never identified.)

Imagine a 2,500 percent reward for sticking by a company you truly loved. Not just *liked* as a consumer of the product; stockholders who had only a lukewarm enthusiasm for the company probably sold out and lost money. In 1982, Johnson & Johnson investors had to have faith that the company could stop a madman from using their product to murder innocent people. Seems easy in hindsight, but it was a very risky call at the time. Wrongful death claims can wipe out corporations.

PASSION ALWAYS WINS

When you love something, when you feel really passionate about it, you'll still be able to sleep restfully at night even when the headlines are screaming at you that the locusts are coming. Fear, anxiety and needing to close the position because you're running out of cash are the three most common ways to lose money on any investment. Investing in what you love conquers two of those in one fell swoop. Being one who says, "Even if it is the end of the world, I'm not going down without my _____ (fill in the blank of your favorite passion that is provided by a publicly traded company)," might get you through enough days to wash ashore to a beautiful island of rich gains.

When you conquer your emotions and the markets pay you for your prescience—that is truly a shot of paradise. That kind of thrill— the same adrenalin rush as winning the lottery—happens all the time with smart investing. The odds are infinitely better on making gains in the stock market than the lottery and are available to you, too, once you rely upon your own base of wisdom and use the disciplines outlined in this book.

THE BOTTOM LINE

Every trick you can use to calm your emotions around stocks gives you an edge that the person next to you doesn't have. Diving into an ocean of love is a lot more enjoyable than drowning in your own stomach acid. Chances are that this approach will also see you living longer to enjoy your wealth as well.

NATALIE'S THREE TAKEAWAY TIPS

Investing in something you care about helps you to:

1. Buy low and sell high because a company you care about is one you won't sell off on the cheap.
2. Keep your radar up for news that helps you to stay current on which company is leading the competition.
3. Use information you already have as a shopper to outperform the pros on Wall Street.

4

HOT INDUSTRIES

*Industrial mutation—if I may use that biological term—
incessantly revolutionizes the economic structure from within,
incessantly destroying the old one, incessantly creating a new
one. This process of Creative Destruction is the essential fact
about capitalism.*

—JOSEPH SCHUMPETER, *Capitalism,
Socialism & Democracy*

Spotting a breakout industry that is poised to pop can be a huge advantage when trying to identify the "leader" and isn't as difficult as you might imagine. For instance, everyone was being told in 2000 that the Internet was a sure shot and that malls were going to be a thing of the past—that's what business was going to be like in the New Economy. Meanwhile, much of the time you couldn't get to the online shopping cart to pay for your items without your computer crashing. Many people with dial-up connections, which represented the majority of the computer users in the United States, had difficulty even accessing some web sites. As a result, almost all of the Internet companies were burning through cash in 2000, not rolling in dough.

Oftentimes when a hot sector is poised to cool off, or vice versa, common sense runs counter to what you're being told by the media or the companies themselves. However, because the people who get to speak on camera on the talk shows are all experts with degrees and well-reasoned arguments, it can be easy to get caught up in their rationale.

Let's take the fad du jour of 2006—ethanol. Self-interested corporations were touting corn as the new home-grown gasoline and were

Figure 4.1. All-electric Tesla Roadster

capturing subsidies in Congress as a result. Meanwhile, some academics warned that the carbon footprint of converting corn to ethanol was bigger than that created by oil and, further, that it was just silly to truck ethanol from the farm fields to the cities in the name of conserving gas.

Whom do you believe? Well, if you did a survey in 2007 asking how many of your neighbors were interested in pumping ethanol into their car, you'd have a pretty low number. If you showed that same group a picture of the Tesla Roadster—an all-electric sports car (Figure 4.1)—you'd see a lot more people leaning forward in their chairs with interest.

Since interest in clean energy was starting to heat up in 2006, you could ask how many neighbors were interested in installing solar panels on their home and come up, again, with a much higher percentage. In fact, there were already many solar-powered products you could pick up at the local home improvement center, which meant that it might be possible for solar companies to start earning profits—something that happened in spades in 2007, when the majority of solar companies went from cash negative to cash positive.

So, which industry turned out to be the most popular in 2007—ethanol, electric car components or solar energy? Solar energy companies performed far above ethanol producers and the general marketplace in both share price gains and increased sales! Clean energy—solar, wind, electric car components, etc.—boasted gains of almost 60 cents on the dollar, compared to the second-highest performing industry—oil and gas—at 32 percent gains. Solar energy companies like Suntech Power Holdings and Sunpower blinded the returns of most corporations on Wall Street with 140 percent and 250 percent gains, respectively.

Meanwhile, Archer Daniels Midland Co., a leading producer of ethanol, followed the market volatility throughout most of 2007 and then posted 45 percent gains in the last quarter of the year. Ethanol, the great hope for reducing our dependency on foreign oil, didn't make a dent in oil and gas prices and was largely responsible for a big increase in food prices in the United States. At the start of 2008, oil prices topped $100 a barrel!

That's how I kept my reign at the top of Wall Street in 2007: by using common sense and some Main Street observations on what people really care about. I didn't rely on complicated charts or chase down interviews with policymakers who were being lobbied to care more about ethanol than solar and electric. I spoke with the smartest people I knew at the most respected economic think tanks and the smartest people I knew down the block, and they were all saying and thinking the exact same thing—that electric cars made more sense than ethanol in the United States and that solar, wind and geothermal were equally interesting as power grid sources because different regions have different sources of abundant renewable energy.

KNOWING WHEN A SECTOR IS RIPE TO BUY

Why did solar and wind energy lie dormant for decades before exploding in 2007? Why did the Internet fail in 2000–2001, but succeed in 2004? Because in the beginning, when innovation is occurring rapidly, the companies are all losing money and have to rely upon venture capital or government support to pay their expenses. It's difficult to predict a clear winner because tomorrow's invention could create a new breakout technology. Additionally, it typically takes two cycles of investments for the innovative idea to become affordable to the masses. As a result, there tend to be a lot more companies that fail than succeed in the first cycle of some industrial or technological innovation.

When you have long periods of capital investment without revenues— long being defined as longer than three years—venture capital providers can get antsy and stop the flow of funds. Young industries that are relying upon government subsidies—as alternative energy was for decades—can lose their funding in the next election. Either scenario is usually enough to grind progress to a halt. That was the case in solar and wind energy for decades (since the late 70s), with Internet stocks in 2000, with the personal-computer bust of the early 80s and even the assembly-line bust in the Great Depression.

A good time to invest in new technology tends to be *after* the initial crash (which is one reason why I was so bullish in 2003 on the second swell of Internet technology companies). The second surge of innovation tends to be longer, more sustained and yields products at attractive price points that help to attract mass consumers. Assembly lines did become a popular production tool. Personal computers did come into every home, and the Internet is rapidly becoming deployed worldwide. It's quite likely that solar energy could follow this trend. But it will require help to get to that tipping point. And the industry continues to struggle with a manufacturing shortage of one of the key elements—silicon.

Green CEOs (as in less experienced) will shine and soar and crash and burn by expanding too fast, over-committing to research and development, missing projections, neglecting to secure capital when they are in good shape and scrambling to obtain high-cost capital when the company is on the ropes. Almost everything spooky about NASDAQ 1999 was creepy about solar energy in 2005, with the exception of a few companies with real earnings, reliable government subsidies and the strongest positions with regard to silicon supply.

In 2006 and going forward, however, the worldwide push toward clean energy has put real earnings in the solar and wind companies and that trend is only beginning. While careful company selection is key, the clean energy industry should continue to lead Wall Street in returns.

As Dr. Charles Zhang, the CEO and chairman of SOHU.com in China, noted in my interview with him in January of 2007, the company that makes the better product will get ten times bigger overnight. Tomorrow's clean energy headline will be about who is harnessing energy faster, cheaper, better with the lowest carbon footprint. The smart companies are innovating, focusing on product, cutting costs and securing basic supplies (like silicon) through long-term contracts. Beware of other companies that might get bogged down in the quarterly earnings reports, since there are so many stakeholders to answer to, or who have to focus on securing capital because they haven't figured out a way to turn a profit yet.

THE BOTTOM LINE

In short, more companies will fail than succeed in hot, new industries, and you have to be very cognizant of which companies are carrying too much debt when considering red-hot, renaissance companies that have been surviving for some time on government subsidies and debt financing, as the solar and wind energy industries have been for decades. The second cycle (after the initial crash and burn of the first cycle) of innovation tends to be longer and more sustained after the product is offered at a reasonable price to the masses.

NATALIE'S THREE TAKEAWAY TIPS

1. New industries are extremely high-risk and volatile because a single breakthrough innovation can create a new industry leader overnight.
2. A good time to invest in new industries tends to be *after* the initial crash.
3. New industries tend to have newbie CEOs. Green CEOs can make all kinds of mistakes in a highly competitive field, so when picking a leader, it pays to notice which company has the most experienced team and board of directors.

5

HITCH YOUR WAGON TO A STAR

There are people who focus on the limitations of the situation, and there are people who focus on the possibilities. The people who focus on the possibilities always achieve more.
—CARLETON S. FIORINA, FORMER CHAIRMAN AND CEO, HEWLETT-PACKARD

As I illustrated in the previous chapter, picking a leading industry is key to laying the groundwork for the next step: selecting the leader of that sector, the company doing the best job within that industry. If you get both of these things right and you buy the company at a good price, then you're very likely to have a rocket ship. And really, the only way that you're going to get both of these things right before everyone else (when the price is still low) is if you know the industry and the company better than anyone else. You'll need to see something there that others are not seeing—yet.

Following, I'll give you some examples of leading companies that I've identified over the years, with a few clues of how I came to that conclusion. This is really an acquired skill so don't get too frustrated if you don't get it right away. By the time you finish this book, you'll be ready to start testing your own wisdom.

Opsware (2002)
Founded by the guy who invented the Web browser, Marc Andreessen, Opsware (formerly LoudCloud) developed software and provisioning management to prevent hackers from compromising enterprise computer systems. An Internet genius had created an indispensable product

that marquee corporations and government agencies were clamoring for. Opsware cracked $100 million in sales by 2006. This company posted up to 690 percent gains from the time I first featured it (in 2002) to the time it was purchased by Hewlett-Packard (in 2007). Incidentally, when I picked this stock on a national television show in 2004, the two well-known stars panned my recommendation of the company.

Rio Tinto (2004)

One of the leading metals mining companies worldwide, Rio Tinto's management had profited during an industry-wide slowdown pre-2003 that had taken most of the competition (including companies with greater name recognition in the United States) deeply into debt. Additionally, Rio Tinto had mines in the most stable countries in the world, avoiding the most volatile regions like Latin America (where nationalization policies can wipe out corporations) and South Africa (where violence was high). I placed Rio Tinto on my Hot News list, when real estate was so hot anyone with a pulse was buying a house, and removed Rio Tinto from my Hot News list when the real estate and building sector started to decline. Copper prices are historically tied to a building boom, and I anticipated a weakening in demand once the real estate run-up subsided. This company earned 145 percent gains between the time I first featured it in May 2004 to the time I took it off the list in November of 2006.

Las Vegas Sands (2005)

This company began building "China's Las Vegas" on the island of Macao in 2004; they owned the beautiful Venetian on the Las Vegas Strip. As an added attraction, the Las Vegas Sands was renowned for building with an eye to husbandry of funds without sacrificing quality, whereas the major competitor in casino resorts typically spent three times the amount on each room without an ability to charge three times the price or give the guests the impression that they were experiencing three times the fun. Las Vegas Sands posted 138 percent gains from the time I featured it in July 2005 to the time I removed it from my Hot News on Cool Stocks list in January 2007.

MySpace (2005)

It's obvious now that MySpace created online social networking. In 2005 the company was already ranking in the top ten most popular sites online and in time spent on the site, even though few people over thirty had heard of it. MySpace also ranked in page views next to Google when MySpace's parent company (Intermix) was trading for under a billion. Meanwhile, Google was carrying over $100 billion in market value. It wasn't hard to predict, even though I was the Lone Ranger at the time, that Rupert Murdoch (or some other media giant) would want to own it. My subscribers made money on MySpace when it was owned by Intermix, as well as after it was purchased by News Corp.

World Water and Power (2007)

Lots of companies make solar panels; few use them to irrigate agricultural fields or to supply potable water to distressed regions like Darfur and the Gulf Coast after Hurricane Katrina. This company held the competitive advantage in a unique application of the hottest industry in the United States—with the ability to attract headlines. The fact that Governor Arnold Schwarzenegger took the CEO on his Green Tour with him in 2007 helped the share price to more than triple in under four months.

While picking the leader of the sector is the trickiest part of this three-ingredient investment recipe, you can go a long way to mastering it by using the Stock Report Card (outlined later in the next chapter), by trying the products and services of the competition before you buy the stock and by asking the four basic questions for determining a leader.

Winning investments have a lot in common with one another, and losing investments tend to be lacking in one or more of four critical areas. Three out of four of the questions I ask to determine the leader can be answered with information you have as a consumer!

The Four Basic Questions for Picking a Leader

1. What's the product? (Let's say Internet/phone/MP3 devices.)
2. Who's going to buy it, and why would they like that product more than the competitor's version? (Why is the Apple iPod more popular than Microsoft's Zune?)
3. Can the company continue to make a superior product now and going forward and get it to the masses while the appetite of their customers is piqued and the product is fresh? (Will Zune or the Blackberry Pearl beat the Apple iPhone in the future?)
4. Who's running the company, and how motivated are the employees to deliver a superior product faster, cheaper, better? (Why do Apple employees love their jobs so much? How did Steve Jobs inspire Pixar to make the best animated films *and* Apple to become the world's most successful music store?)

An extraordinary number of things have to go right within a company for a superior product or service to show up in the stores at a reasonable price. If a company is doing enough right to get you to come to them and buy their product, a thousand things have gone right from the executive suite down to the shipping dock and over to the accounts receivable department. If you're choosing their product over the competition, you have a good understanding of why. And most of this research involves something many of us love: shopping. Not one mind-numbing chart.

Google Mania

In 2004, Google launched its Initial Public Offering but had only a billion dollars in annual sales. The financial pundits appearing on the national news shows with me were naturally comparing Google to the second-place winner in search, Yahoo. Most posited that Google could never manage to match Yahoo's $33 billion valuation. They thought that Google was no Yahoo and never would be—even though Google was the top search engine—because Yahoo was the leading Internet services provider with a lot of diversified interests, including online gaming, e-mail and more. Google was only search.

Google had survived the dot-com crash and, like Yahoo and eBay, was profitable. But should a company with just $1 billion in sales come out of the box with a $33 billion (or higher) market valuation and a 33 price-earnings ratio—especially when investors were still smarting from the 2000–2002 dot-com recession? Would the Google mania of individual investors push the share price into the obscene?

Google had become the talk over the water cooler. Everyone was abuzz that they could own a piece of their beloved search engine, because the "Dutch Auction" was designed to allow common investors the chance to bid and win IPO shares. For one of the few times in history, the average, individual investor was getting a shot at owning her favorite company *before* it began trading on the big boards.

All of this chaos and the unconventional business strategies, including the "triumvirate" power structure of the two founders and the new CEO, Dr. Eric Schmidt, and Google's online mandate to "never do evil," gave most analysts plenty of oddities to rant about. A web site calling itself "google-watch.org" showed the company's logo in flames, accompanied by a screaming headline that proclaimed:

Ten reasons why you should drop
everything and go to your bank,

withdraw all the money you
saved for Google's IPO,

go home and stuff it
under your mattress,

and sit on it!

I was one of the few who looked at all of the peculiarities, peered deeper into Google's innovative and diversified revenue stream and ferreted out the skyrocketing growth trends of online advertising. My enthusiasm for Google began from answering my Four Questions. After my initial pre-screening, using these four questions, I verified that there was indeed a migration of print magazine and newspaper advertising dollars (even from stalwarts like *Forbes* and *The New York Times*) to Internet advertising. I also confirmed that Google had managed to tap into the mom-and-pop-shop advertising market, stealing revenue from the Yellow Pages, where small businesses advertise in good times *and* bad to keep the flow of customers coming their way.

Here's what that analysis looked like:

The Four Basic Questions for Picking Winning Stocks

1. What's the product?

Search engine. Something we all need and use daily, to the point that "Google it" has become part of the language. (You don't hear anyone saying "Yahoo it," do you?) Plus most of us hated pop-up ads. Google never had them. The other leading web sites did and were annoying the heck out of their customers.

2. Who's going to buy it, and why would they like that product more than the competitor's version?

The Google web site was used for 34 percent of Internet searches in the United States in February 2004, according to ComScore Networks, ahead of Yahoo (30 percent) and MSN (15 percent). Google was also the number-one search engine in the UK, Germany, France, Italy, Netherlands, Spain, Switzerland and Australia, with 81.9 million global unique users per month. Why did users like the product better? It was a better search engine, returning dozens more pertinent options per inquiry than the competition. Additionally, they developed easy-to-use text ads, which looked pleasingly similar to the responses to your search query. And, again, there were none of the dreaded pop-up ads.

3. Can the company make a superior product and get it to the masses while the customer's appetite is piqued and the product is fresh?

Google had been leading search queries online for so long that it had become a pop phenomenon. Just as Kleenex has become a generic term for tissue, Google has come to mean "search," regardless of which search engine is being used. Whenever a company achieves that level of supremacy, they are more difficult to displace because, without advertising, their brand is handed down generation to generation by word of mouth. Additionally, Google made it easy for smaller, local mom-and-pop companies to capture a part of the global search marketplace (and a little revenue stream of their own), while beautifying the Google bottom line. Google is entrenched in the American lifestyle, as well as in many nations around the globe.

4. Who's running the company, and how motivated are the employees to deliver superior product faster, cheaper, better?

The two guys who founded Google were young, energetic Stanford graduate students. The experienced Internet CEO they hired to oversee the business agreed to be involved in a "triumvirate" of power, which meant that the sensible energy that had brought a billion dollars in revenue to the company would still carry weight. The three executives required engineers to spend a day a week on projects that interested them, unrelated to their day jobs. The Google reception area was decorated with lava lamps and beanbag chairs. The founders regularly skated in the biweekly roller hockey game during lunchtime. Employees were known to gain the "Google 20"—twenty pounds they put on because Google offers free food to their staff members. And the company promised to make money without being evil. Lofty goals perhaps, but it certainly seemed to be working.

I have a motto that says, "Happy people make better products faster, cheaper." Google's book on success might very well bear that title.

WHAT'S THE SCORE?

If I were scoring each of the four questions, Google would have ranked an A+ in all four. As such, I predicted on May 1, 2004: "I don't need to tell you that if the editors of *American Heritage* are forced to include a noun as a verb in the dictionary, you're witnessing an historic phenomenon. . . . Google continues to break the mold and is committed to continuing that trend with an unprecedented IPO, which is likely to become one of the most successful IPO's ever."

Google *did* in fact post the most successful launch for a public company ever. By May 2006, the company had a valuation of $136 billion. Dr. Eric Schmidt has the distinction of being the only CEO to take a company from IPO to over $136 billion in market capitalization in under two years.

Readers of my e-zine who heeded my reporting and bought Google at the IPO were dancing on the ceiling by 2007. By the end of

2007, Google was worth more than 200 billion dollars, with $12 billion in annual sales. By comparison, Yahoo had grown from a $33 billion market capitalization to a very modest $44 billion, with annual sales of $6.5 billion. Google's share price rocketed from the initial public offering price of $85 to $747 per share at its high in 2007.

What's more important for our analytical purposes is that these four questions work. Most of the analysts and money managers who appeared with me on national television shows in May 2004 were stuck in the earnings reports and weren't focused on the growth potential (of the company or of the Internet) or the power and weight of Google in pop culture. They had no way of measuring just how hard happy employees will work to make their beloved corporation very successful.

Now, let's compare Google with a company that was on my Cooling Off list from 2004 to 2007—General Motors. In my July 1, 2004, article, "Hybrids: Car of the Stars, But Should You Own the Stock?" I warned that General Motors and Ford were going to hit tough times. In that article, I predicted, "Good-bye SUVs" and hello hybrids.

We knew about global warming at that time—an ice sheet the size of Rhode Island had fallen off of Antarctica—though there were many who were still trying to deny it. Honda and Toyota had made a large investment in hybrids and alternative energy cars while General Motors was still backing research and development in hydrogen fuel cells and had a *substantial* production commitment to large trucks and SUVs. Here's how the Four Questions applied to GM:

1. *What's the product?*

In early 2004, before the heart-stopping spike in oil and gas prices, GM was producing mostly SUVs and Hummers while Toyota and Honda were promoting the new hybrids. General Motors had production lines that were committed to continuing the production of SUVs because SUVs were still testing well in focus groups, while Honda and

Toyota had the vision to understand that hybrids were the wave of the future, even if the soccer moms of America didn't know that yet. The Toyota Prius Hybrid was even named Motor Trend's Car of the Year in 2004.

2. Who's going to buy it, and why would they like that product more than the competitor's version?

After gas prices jumped, the bottom fell out of the market for SUVs and Hummers, but even prior to that, you could see and feel the growing wave of concern over global warming. It was no accident that Motor Trend picked a hybrid to be the Car of the Year in 2004. Celebrities were arriving at the Academy Awards in hybrids. The stigma of driving gas guzzlers was something that could sink a career. Within two years, California Governor Arnold Schwarzenegger, the Governator, had to install a hydrogen fuel cell into his Hummer so that he wouldn't be perceived as a hypocrite—promoting "green" while his car guzzled gas like water. Everyone ran hard and fast to fuel-efficient vehicles, while GM was stuck in union talks, losing billions of dollars and struggling to revamp production lines.

3. Can the company make a superior product and get it to the masses while the customer's appetite is piqued and the product is fresh?

A big part of the problem with General Motors was vision. If the company had the vision to invest in hybrids and smaller cars, even when the focus group data was counter to that, Toyota might not have topped General Motors in sales. Another part of the problem, however, and one that was easier to see, was that "Generous" Motors was having trouble getting their costs under control. The cost of certain goods, like metals, had tripled, causing an industry-wide concern that wasn't unique to GM. However, the cost of labor for GM, at 25 cents out of every dollar sold, was the highest in the industry, except for Ford. There were many news reports that GM was putting a lot of pressure on the pension managers in the company to earn excessively high gains to help the bottom line—a risky practice that is counter to how the retirement plans of any company or individual should be run. Delphi, a former parts division of GM, was teetering on the edge of bankruptcy. You can easily see how with all of these challenges, the CEO at GM was not focusing on leading the industry with new product ideas.

How could you uncover all this stuff about pension plans and labor unions and costs out of control? Well, you can access the earning reports at SEC.gov and power-search the documents, using the key words "pension," "Other Post Employment Benefits" (or "OPEB"), "debt," "risk" and "liability." By going straight to the areas of concern, you could have found out almost everything you needed to know in just a few easy minutes. Also, the high costs, pension difficulties, labor union talks and other red flags were making headlines.

4. Who's running the company, and how motivated are the employees to deliver superior product faster, cheaper, better?

The CEOs of both Ford and General Motors are respected in the industry for having to do a very hard job, steering these legacy corporations through some of the same challenges that forced so many airlines to go into bankruptcy—high materials costs, high labor costs and crushing debt obligations to pensions and health care for their retirees (those OPEBs). Ford and GM both faced a global market that constrained their ability to price their product higher. On the other hand, GM was rightfully criticized for not switching to fuel-efficient cars more quickly.

Unfortunately, in a stormy climate of salary slashing and benefit slicing and dicing, staff morale typically drowns. It's tough on your smile when you get your pay cut or your benefits reduced, and it takes a saint not to want to blame the boss who's running the company for the tough times. In that climate, General Motor's Chairman and CEO

Rick Wagoner had his work cut out for him just to keep the company in business. Making the business profitable would require a multiyear turnaround strategy.

WINNER OR LOSER?

If I were scoring all four questions for General Motors, the company gets Ds across the board. In July 2004, I warned to stay away from the entire auto industry and General Motors in particular. Over the next three years, General Motors remained on my Cooling Off list. By May 2007, with $94 billion owed in long-term debt, pensions and OPEBs, General Motors owed over five times more in debt obligations than the $18 billion market value of the company.

From 2004 to 2007, Google returned almost nine dollars for every dollar invested, while General Motors' investors lost more than 30 cents on each dollar invested, making Google the clear winner.

THE BOTTOM LINE

If you have an idea where the shopper is voting with her dollars and her feet—and you know why—you actually have a leg up on the Wall Street analyst who cannot veer too dramatically from the schooled system of analysis. Again, you can see the trends in the stores months before those trends show up in the earnings report (and on the analyst's desk). If a company is adept at "managing earnings," that is, parceling out problem areas over a few earnings periods—as the telecommunications companies that went bankrupt in 2002–2003 did—then you're seeing consumer trends *many months* before the analysts on Wall Street. It didn't take a genius to see that long distance rates had fallen from 25 cents per minute to four cents per minute (and zero if you were using the Internet for your long distance calls). Just like small business, when big business prices are slashed severely overnight, that's very bad news for profits.

So, if you can pick good fruit at the supermarket, you can apply those same skills, under the framework of the Four Questions, to select the quality goods (and weed out the duds) at the stock market, too.

NATALIE'S THREE TAKEAWAY TIPS

1. Three out of four questions to pick the star company in an industry can be answered by information you have as a shopper.
2. As a consumer, you are getting information about the product and product sales firsthand months before the data lands on an analyst's desk.
3. Happy people make better products faster and cheaper.

6

THE MAGIC OF
STOCK REPORT CARDS

Investing without research is like playing stud poker and never looking at the cards.
—PETER LYNCH

So you're going to invest in what you know and love, and then you're going to pick the leader in its sector. In real estate, the leader is as easy as "location, location, location." But how do you spot a leader on Wall Street? Exactly how are you supposed to factor a customer service representative's sunny disposition or a pleasant shopping experience into an evaluation of whether a company's stock is going to rise?

I've given you a solid background for how you can use your expertise as a shopper to put you on the road to finding the sector leader, but there are still some hidden factors that I've discussed only cursorily—such as sales, pension plan debt, other post-employment benefits (OPEBs), income and others. This important data is like an EKG to check up on the health of the company. The more crushing the demands of operating, the less time the executives have to dream up cool new things to offer their customers.

Don't worry about all of these acronyms! My Stock Report Card, which we'll get to shortly, makes it easy to line up the numbers, easy to see what really matters and easy to tell which corporation is drowning in debt or swimming in profits!

INTUITION: COMPLICATED PATTERN RECOGNITION

In the past, you might have had a hunch about something and wanted to act on it but feared basing a financial decision on nothing more than your intuition. Great instinct. You should never make any financial decision on just one piece of information, any more than you would try to guess a picture by looking at just one piece of a 100-piece puzzle.

I'm not telling you to ignore your intuition; I just want you to recognize it as being only part of the equation. We know now more about how the brain works and what intuition really is: complicated pattern recognition or the ability to assimilate seemingly unrelated bits of data into useable information. (Think of how a detective learns to sniff out a lie by observing the body language of a suspect, or how your mother was always good at knowing when you had been to a party.)

Your brain has stored all kinds of memories. As you gain time and experience on this planet, you learn how to tell if someone is conning you, if the person you're talking to seems happy, sad or angry, no matter what they're saying to you, as well as who among your coworkers is working hard and who's hardly working and so on. The process we call intuition is simply your subconscious telling you something based upon recall of past experiences with similar circumstances.

When a wise old woman scrunches her eyes at her granddaughter's fiancée disapprovingly, she is utilizing decades of wisdom and experience to read the signposts of his soul, which are written upon everything from the way he can't look her in the eye, to the premature wrinkles, to the tattoos, to the dark circles under his eyes. The picture before her is not auspicious and she says so, with confidence, to anyone willing to listen, that her granddaughter deserves better.

She has a million reasons for her conclusions, if you're willing to hear them. It is not just a hunch.

How many times have you thought, "I knew I should have invested in that!" You had this or that hunch and, sure enough, when the markets get hot and everyone's "in the money," you kick yourself because you could have made a killing. Well, you would have been smart to take heed of your hunch and employ the Stock Report Card to line up the competition and make sure that you're picking a winner. Successful investing is never simply shooting from the hip.

INTUITION IN ACTION

My intuition is a large part of how I came up with the general guideline that when CEOs are suing instead of competing, their products will become less interesting and they will lose market share. Instead of being hyper-focused on thrilling the customer with better products and services, the head of the corporation is diverting her attention to battling with the competition. Take a look at MVP NBA players, like Kobe Bryant, and you'll see that his eyes are on the basket when he scores. He charges right past the guards and focuses solely on getting the ball through the hoop—come what may. Suing is akin to taking your eye off the basket and dribbling around endlessly, which is very risky (especially since the clock can run out).

I'm embarrassed to admit that I learned this firsthand. As a young singer, I had a record company that used my voice and keyboard playing on a record without paying me what they were contracted to pay me. I wasted a year in court, at the urging of my attorney, who promised that we were talking really big sums of money. All I ended up winning was a six-month stay in the record executive's roach-ridden apartment building that he owned. In the meantime, a year of valuable youth flew by, and Madonna had become the next big thing!

In fact, any time I see an executive complaining instead of conquering, I take that as a big red flag that the company is going to have problems keeping up with the competition. Overstock.com was a company I featured at $11.50 in 2002 and then took off the Hot List at $55 per share in 2005 when the CEO tried to sue hedge fund managers for shorting his stock. Overstock's CEO was actually using valuable television time to talk about the justice of the lawsuit instead of why Overstock was the best place online to buy things (better than their competitor, Amazon.com). Whether he had a right to sue, as I felt when I had been grievously abused by the record company, is quite beside the point when you are losing customers and money.

In September 2007, the share price of Overstock.com was still half (at $26) of what it was when I took it off of my Hot News on Cool Stocks list, and the company was struggling to maintain market share while taking on more debt to keep operating. While they did win a few battles in the courtroom and were given the green light by the California Supreme Court to proceed with a lawsuit against Gradient Analytics and Rocker Partners in 2007, whom Overstock claims conspired to drive down the value of its stock, they weren't winning the game for customers and share price gains. I'm sure investors and customers alike wish the company gained headlines for products, not lawsuits.

I staked the same claim in 2007 when Advanced Micro Devices tried to sue Intel into submission, telling my readers, "AMD's strategy of litigate to win, loses, in our view. In technology, the geeks beat the suits." The best product, not the winning lawsuit, attracts customers. During 2007, Intel posted up to 40 percent gains, while Advanced Micro Devices lost money for its investors.

As you honor your particular observations and begin testing them, you might have the same kind of success in identifying the destructive tendencies of CEOs who will have their companies stumbling in the race of the competitive marketplace. With stock picking, clues that you pick up—again, sometimes without even being aware—can be a valuable addition to the assembling of hard facts, provided you don't rely upon that one piece of information as the complete picture. If something sits well in my gut, that's a great start, but it's only one bit of information on the Stock Report Card.

Are you prepared to defend your investments? Have you really got twenty great reasons why you just bought stock in XYZ Company? Do you even have ten? And if you consider the Three Ingredient

---

ESSENTIAL FINANCIAL TERMS

Before diving in to see how my Stock Report Card works, here are some terms you'll want to familiarize yourself with.

ADR (American Depositary Receipt): This is how foreign companies trade on the U.S. stock exchanges. An ADR is a negotiable certificate issued by a U.S. bank representing a specific number of shares of a foreign company.

P/E (Price-to-Earnings Ratio): This is the price of a stock divided by its earnings per share. It tells you how expensive the company's stock is. A listing of "N/A" means that the company is losing money. It's not uncommon for a new company or a company that is going through restructuring to lose money while it ramps up for new sales. General Motors lost money in 2006 and 2007—major restructuring—and so did Wisdom Tree, a new exchange-traded funds company with some of the top business leaders on Wall Street involved in the management and advisement of the company.

Earnings per share: The earnings of the company divided by the number of shares outstanding. For instance, a corporation with $100 million in earnings and 100 million shares outstanding would report earnings per share of $1.

Sales and income: Be sure to check both of these statistics. A company could have a lot of sales but still be losing money in income because the expenses are higher than the money the corporation is bringing in. Additionally, rising trends in sales and earnings are positive signs, whereas losing trends can be a sign of continued trouble ahead.

Recipe, have you covered each area thoroughly? Do you really know the company and the product and why you love it more than the competition? Do you really believe that the product you are investing in will continue to be the best in the marketplace going forward? Why? Are you buying it at a good price?

Remember that grandmother. Be like her—steely-eyed and on the lookout for flaws—when you size up any potential investment. After

---

ESSENTIAL FINANCIAL TERMS, *continued*

52-week high and low: Check the annual low and high prices to get a perspective on whether or not you're buying high on the year. Many sites also allow you to construct historical charts of the share price with one easy click. You can look at the history of the company's share price for the past five to ten years and more very easily online.

Market capitalization and number of shares outstanding: The market value of a company is the product of the share price and the total number of common shares. Multibillion dollar corporations provide stability for your portfolio and are less likely to have huge price fluctuations (either up or down). Companies with a smaller market capitalization, under one billion, perform better on average than the rest of the marketplace, but they also have a higher risk attached to that performance.

D/E (Debt/Equity Ratio): This is the total long-term debt compared to the market capitalization of the company. Extremely high D/Es could indicate that the industry, sector or company is not doing very well. If you see N/A in this column on the financial site's stock page, go to the most recent earnings report on the SEC's web site (SEC.gov) to find out the long-term debt, which is likely to be quite large. (Companies without any debt put 00.00 in the D/E column.)

Institutional investors: Institutional investors move the markets. If you've found a company before the analysts discover it, you could benefit from increased institutional investors' interest.

Operating margins: This is the difference between the cost of goods (net income) and the price the company is able to charge for the product or service (net sales).

you ask the four questions to pick the leader, start filling out the Stock Report Card, lining up the numbers of the competition alongside the company you suspect will bear out as the winning investment. See if the numbers reinforce that vision or tell a different story.

THE STOCK REPORT CARD

The Stock Report Card provides an organized way of looking at the key indicators of a company's sales, profit margins, debt, insider trading, price-to-earnings ratio and more. When you line up the numbers, the whole story starts making a lot more sense. It's by using this method that I've had such success at picking winners, like Taser International, my 2003 Company of the Year, which went on to rack up to 9,000 percent returns for investors after my feature article. There are a lot of gains to be made by learning how to pick the leader in the sector. My Stock Report Card is basically a table in which I enter information about the companies in the sector I'm exploring. These are the items I gather:

Company	Symbol	P/E	Price	52-wk Low & High	Sales; Income	Market Cap; # Shares	Debt/ Equity Ratio	Insider Trading	Operating Margins

The first two columns are simple enough—the name of the company and its listing symbol on the stock market pages and web sites. (You can get the stock symbol easily by Googling with a search on the company name and the words "stock symbol.")

The next column, P/E, is the cost of a share of stock divided by the earnings per share.

In the next two columns, I list the current price and the high and low prices during the preceding 52 weeks—to get a sense of where

---

NATALIE'S NOTE

The more popular the company, the more it will cost you relative to earnings for each share you buy. A P/E of 100 means that investors are paying 100 times more than the company is earning (on a per share basis). A P/E of 20 means that the company is earning $1 per share, but investors are willing to pay 20 times that for each share of the company. A P/E lower than 15 could indicate that the stock is "on sale"; that is, less popular or trading at a good value. A high P/E might indicate a very popular company (Apple Computer's P/E was 39 on September 20, 2007) or a younger, growth company (like SunPower, which in the spring of 2007 had a P/E of 135— though this was much lower than the 638 P/E of the previous October).

---

the stock is trading relative to the price during the year. (It doesn't hurt to construct a five- or ten-year chart as well, which can be done on most financial web sites with two clicks.)

I put the company's annual sales and its annual income into the next column, allowing me to see the two numbers at a glance. A company will sometimes have sales that look great but have crushing costs (as General Motors had in 2006–2008), creating negative income that, if sustained, could threaten to put the company out of business.

Next comes market capitalization—which you can think of as the total value that investors have placed on the company—and the number of shares outstanding.

The debt/equity ratio is a vital clue as to whether the company is burdened by excessive debt. Look for the number to be smaller than 0.5, which means 50 percent of the market value. Any number above 1.5 should raise concern, and double-digit numbers are a red flag.

The insider trading figures reveal whether top company executives and major investors are buying more stock in the firm or unloading their shares. And operating margins give a sense of whether the company is able to get a significant mark-up for their goods and services.

All of this data is available from your favorite financial web site. You can also click through to this information easily from my web site. Simply go to NataliePace.com, enter the stock symbol in the Company Research box and click on "Research Now." (You can use this same strategy to find out the holdings in your mutual funds.)

For the three companies in the solar industry that were the most popular and promising at the time, here's the data I assembled:

STOCK REPORT CARD, SOLAR ENERGY, OCTOBER 2006

Company	Symbol	P/E	Price	52-wk Low & High	Sales; Income	Market Cap; # Shares	Debt/ Equity Ratio	Insider Trading	Operating Margins
Evergreen Solar	ESLR	N/A	$8.30	17.50/ 7.74	57.13 M -25.20 M	557.3 M 67.15 M	1.41	$6.5 M sold	-26.68
SunPower Solar	SPWR	638.70	$27.74	45.09/ 23.75	147.90 M 3.37 M	1.912 B 68.91 M	00.00	$8.5 M sold	11.21
Suntech Power Holdings	STP	65.10	$25.83	45.95/ 19.00	226 M .6 M	3.853 B 149.2 M	.19	Not Known	17.3

As a first step in evaluating the data, I start by sorting the table by price-earnings ratio, lower to higher. After this sorting, the chart then looks like this:

STOCK REPORT CARD, SOLAR ENERGY,
OCTOBER 2006 SORTED BY P/E

Company	Symbol	P/E	Price	52-wk Low & High	Sales; Income	Market Cap; # Shares	Debt/ Equity Ratio	Insider Trading	Operating Margins
Suntech Power- Holdings	STP	65.10	$25.83	45.95/ 19.00	226 M .6 M	3.853 B 149.2 M	.19	Not Known	17.3
SunPower Solar	SPWR	638.70	$27.74	45.09/ 23.75	147.90 M 3.37 M	1.912 B 68.91 M	00.00	$8.5 M sold	11.21
Evergreen Solar	ESLR	N/A	$8.30	17.50/ 7.74	57.13 M -25.20 M	557.3 M 67.15 M	1.41	$6.5 M sold	-26.68

As you can see, Suntech clearly stood out as the bargain leader in terms of having the lowest share price with respect to earnings. Suntech's low P/E was a strong positive indicator. Typically, companies in young industries are still losing money for the first few years of operations while the astronomical costs of research and development exceed the low prices they must sell their products at.

NATALIE'S NOTE

Many financial web pages show "N/A" (not available) for the price-earnings ratio when a company is operating at a loss— that is, when the earnings are negative. Since N/A P/E equals negative earnings, I list the N/A companies last. Anytime you see N/A listed for debt equity or P/E, you need to refer to the original earnings report for the exact numbers and assume that the number is a negative number (that the company is losing money).

SunPower's P/E of 638 may sound very high, but it's somewhat misleading—and this illustrates just how much skill and experience is needed to properly understand and evaluate P/E, which is why you shouldn't be overly reliant on this measure as the sole determination of price. A high number like this isn't uncommon for an innovative young company that's doubling their sales every six months, as Sun-Power was doing at the time. For instance, Google's P/E was negative at their IPO, but just three years and $172 billion later was in the 46 P/E range.

Evergreen Solar was losing money, as indicated by the N/A in the price-earnings column and the negative $25 million in the Income listing. With losses of $25 million, compared to income in both of the other companies, you can see that Evergreen was limping along compared to the competition. This observation becomes key as we continue our analysis. Remember: all impediments to winning the race to have the best product and the highest operating margins foreshadow the future challenges of the company.

Now, even though Evergreen looked to be at a disadvantage to the other two on this stock report card, the company had been the darling of the headlines in the previous year, and there is a tendency to think that if they can make those kinds of headlines in the past, they might do it in the future. So, I say Evergreen looks to be the laggard, but the story isn't quite that simple. This was the company installing solar panels on the roofs of government buildings in Washington, D.C. Somebody in the company had some decent business connections and might be a White Knight for the company, since subsidies were still key to the future of solar energy at that time.

The next things I look at are sales and income. In any industry, when the sales of a number of companies are doubling, you're looking at a basket of stocks that you want to own. (During the Internet bubble, sales weren't doubling; *share prices* were doubling. People bought the story of the New Economy, but the companies hadn't yet figured out how to charge for services and products on web sites.) More and more nations, homeowners, builders, architects, city planners and corporations were incorporating solar energy into their designs. In the Sales and Income column, again you can see that Suntech is the undisputed leader, with over double the sales and twenty times the income of the nearest competitor, SunPower.

From my online research, I also found that Suntech's revenue had been doubling every year—from $85 million in 2004, to well over $200 million in 2005, to a (then) projected $571 million in 2006. SunPower grew like mad as well, from $11 million in 2004 to well over $200 million in 2006. Evergreen Solar rang up the least amount of sales, at $103 million for 2006. It was also burdened with the highest debt load; this is shown in the "Debt/Equity ratio" column, which reveals the amount of long-term debt in proportion to the market capitalization (or value) of the company.

"Insider Trading" allows you to peek into what the company's top executives and major stockholders are doing with their shares—which sometimes gives a clue to their thinking about the upcoming prospects of the firm. (This kind of disclosed trading by the executives and directors of the corporation is legal. Illegal insider trading is when company executives and directors try to buy or sell on information that the public does not have access to.)

With a young company, selling by insiders near the Initial Public Offering can mean that they are simply taking advantage of the company's success so far to put some cash back in their pockets. (Google founders cashed out multimillions at the IPO but still had billions remaining in their company. Since they had likely spent more than a night or two on someone's couch while they were developing the company, who can blame them for cashing in some of their holdings?) With a more established firm or if the company has been public for some time, colossal consensus insider selling can be a red flag that the stock price may be about to sink. Enron executives were cashing out by the multimillions before that company went down. (Monster selling by one lone executive could also just be portfolio diversification.)

In my study of the solar energy companies, there weren't any red flags for insider trading.

And finally, operating margins can show you which company has a competitive edge in profitability. In these days of a global market-place, a company based out of China should have lower labor expenses. The operating margins statistic, which is also available on the financial page of most money web sites, gives you an overview of who has the competitive operating advantage in one easy number. Here again, one company established itself as the leader while another was clearly bringing up the rear.

The small amount of time you spend to construct this chart simply makes it easier to view all of the data in one snapshot. It's a very easy process. When you line up the numbers, as you can see in this case, they start pointing to one leader in the pack. I'm always amazed at how much the leader reliably outshines the competition on the Stock Report Card. Other stock pickers, money managers and even some analysts who are less meticulous simply picked the company in the news, which is the clear laggard on the Stock Report Card.

Suntech was the leader in P/E and sales, as well as income and operating margins, and had very low debt. Meanwhile, Evergreen Solar was losing money, was processing fewer orders and—as revealed by the debt figure—was obviously taking on debt to stay in business while the executives presumably struggled to gain market share and improve operating margins.

The numbers were all pointing to Suntech Power Holdings as the leader in the sector, but the numbers don't give the whole story. If Suntech had just lost its CEO, or was being investigated by the SEC, or had had an explosion at a factory, the setback could impact its ability to maintain a lead on its competitors in the future. To find out what's been happening lately, I move on to the next phase of my research: gathering recent news on the company.

See the following page for the News and Comments section of my solar industry Stock Report Card from October 2006. I list the companies alphabetically so that I can evaluate the news rather than be influenced by the preference I've already begun forming.

INDUSTRY REPORT CARD, SOLAR ENERGY, OCTOBER 2006
NEWS AND COMMENTS

Hmmm. One thing is clear: Solar energy is heating up. Every one of these companies has something good going on (unlike the airline sector at the time, when most of the airlines were struggling every quarter to make ends meet). But which company is truly the leader in the sector, when everyone is claiming to have a strong pipeline of orders, new technology, reliable access to silicon supplies and an edge with institutional investors?

One of the most important factors revealed in the News section was that Suntech was the only company on the chart with a guarantee of silicon in the first half of 2007—yet another sign that this company was likely to solidify its place as a leader. SunPower and Evergreen had secured deals but didn't expect to see full production capacity until the second half of 2007—and only then if the new facilities got to full-capacity manufacturing on time with no snags. Anyone who has ever remodeled knows that delays and budget overages are fairly commonplace. Because of the silicon shortage, failure to meet production orders could impact all of the deals announced by both companies.

Normally, you'd get excited about a listing on the Russell Index because that could mean that institutional investors might be buying in, and obviously a strong wave of investment pushes the price up. But

Evergreen Solar: Develops, manufactures and markets solar power products that provide reliable and environmentally clean electric power throughout the world. Wafer, cell and module manufacturing with patents in all three areas.	Revenues were up 106 percent in 2006 over 2005, to $22 million from $10.7 million, but choked silicon supplies are expected to constrain growth in 2007 to 10 percent, even with backlogs. Net loss for the second quarter of 2006 was $7.5 million. When polysilicon manufacturer MEMC Electronic Materials, Inc. backed out of a deal to supply the material to Evergreen in March 2006, the solar panel company saw its shares shed nearly 19 percent over the next two trading days. On November 4, 2005, Evergreen announced a $70 million sales agreement with PowerLight Corporation that could go up to $170 million. Evergreen's patented String Ribbon wafer technology enables the company to manufacture solar wafers, cells and modules more efficiently than conventional methods and generates nearly one-and-a-half times as much power per pound of refined silicon as conventional methods, according to the company. Evergreen is constructing a plant in Thalheim, Germany, and is on track to reach full production capacity by the end of the third quarter of 2006. ESLR joined the Russell 2000 and Russell 3000 indices on June 24, 2005. These are indices that many institutional investors buy into; a very good sign. Signed a five-year, approximately $200 million deal with SunEdison, LLC, which is Evergreen's fifth major contract secured since November 2005.
Sunpower Solar: Manufactures solar cells, solar panels and inverters that convert sunlight to electricity. The company is currently focusing on residential and commercial applications. In addition, the company makes imaging detectors based on its solar power technology, primarily for medical imaging applications. Began production in late 2004.	Revenue up 233 percent in 2nd quarter 2006 over 2nd quarter 2005. SunPower announced on September 29, 2006, that it will invest in a joint venture with Woongjin Coway to manufacture mono-crystalline silicon ingots. This joint venture will operate in Korea with polysilicon to be supplied primarily from DC Chemical, Korea's largest chemical company. SunPower expects to purchase approximately $250 million of silicon ingot. Manufacturing should begin in the second half of 2007. SunPower's president/chief technology officer was awarded the prestigious Becquerel Prize for Outstanding Merits in Photovoltaics at the 21st European Photovoltaic Solar Energy Conference, Dresden, Germany, in 2006. The University of Colorado, champion of the first Department of Energy's Solar Decathlon, chose to use SunPower to defend their title in 2005 and won.
Suntech Power Holdings (ADR): Founded in January of 2001 by Dr. Zhengrong Shi, a distinguished PV technology scientist, Suntech has rapidly developed into a leading solar energy company. In less than three years after it commenced business operations in May 2002, Suntech increased its manufacturing capacity twelve-fold, and became one of the world's top ten manufacturers of PV cells based on production output.	IPO December 2005. Total net revenues for the second quarter of 2006 were $128.2 million, an increase of 42.6 percent sequentially and 205 percent year-over-year. Suntech began to sell PV cells and modules into several new markets during the second quarter of 2006, including France, Greece and Portugal and saw strong sales growth in the United States and Chinese markets. Suntech's required silicon supply for planned production in 2007 has been fully secured through long-term supply contracts with MEMC, OEM exchange programs and strategic alliances with key suppliers. On May 19, 2005, Suntech completed the acquisition of 100 percent of the voting interests in Wuxi Suntech Power Co., Ltd. The acquisition of MSK Corporation, one of Japan's largest PV module manufacturers and one of the top-ranking companies in the building-integrated photovoltaics space, gives STP a strong presence in the Japanese market. Dr. Zhengrong Shi, Suntech's chairman and CEO, is a member of the International Advisory Committee of the New York Stock Exchange (meaning that he'll continue to gain more visibility with U.S. institutional investors).

with so many other factors going against Evergreen, this one bit of information wasn't enough to change my view.

If you picked Suntech as the leader, you are developing your eye for leaders. The line of reasoning I've just taken you through led me to name Suntech Power Holdings as my feature company in October of 2006 (and later as the 2007 Company of the Year). I wrote, "With the largest market capitalization, the highest sales (double that of SunPower's), the lowest price-to-earnings ratio, a corner on the silicon market and a Chinese labor force, it's difficult to imagine that any American-based solar energy company will catch up to Suntech's colossal lead. During this decade, solar energy may at long last become a viable renewable energy alternative, and if it does, you'll be glad you purchased your SunTech shares this year."

So how did my selection work out?

Friday, March 2, 2007, capped the worst weeks on Wall Street since 9/11. The Dow Jones Industrial Average lost 447 points that week—with the biggest losses concentrated in Chinese stocks. (Uh Oh.) July 2007 was another challenging month in stocks, when the first wave of subprime mortgage foreclosures caused jitters that had nervous investors selling off in droves.

SOLAR ENERGY COMPANIES

PRICE PERFORMANCE, OCTOBER 2006 TO AUGUST 2007

Company	Symbol	Price 9.29.06	Price 7.20.07	Percent Gain
Suntech Power Holdings	STP	$25.83	$42.34	+64
SunPower Solar	SPWR	$27.74	$67.94	+145
Evergreen Solar	ESLR	$8.30	$9.34	+12.5

Yes, SunPower did even better over that period, but in late 2007, *Time* magazine named Suntech's Chairman and CEO Dr. Shi as one of their Heroes of the Environment. Suntech's share price popped up to $90—for returns of more than three times the investment.

The laggard we identified—Evergreen—performed far beneath the rest of the industry.

THE BOTTOM LINE

I know you're ready for a Mojito now, but this process will center your research discipline and become much easier over time. So, become friendly with the Stock Report Card and utilize it religiously as your reality check every time you receive a hot tip or read an article about a company that you're interested in. This template will identify the information that you're missing and will remind you to fill in the pieces of the puzzle before putting your hard-earned money on the line. It will also make you feel more confident that you've done your homework and selected a great company in the event that the markets or the company hit temporary bad news that negatively impacts the share price.

Blank report cards can be downloaded from NataliePace.com. Simply click on "Investor Edu," and select "Stock Report Cards" to access.

NATALIE'S THREE TAKEAWAY TIPS

1. The more crushing the demands of operating, the less time the executives have to dream up cool new things to offer their customers. Even today's leaders can fall behind if the company is losing money, if the workers are walking out or if the executives are buried in lawsuits.

2. The Stock Report Card makes it easy to line up the numbers, easy to see what really matters and easy to tell which corporation is drowning in debt, swimming in profits and trading for a song. And it helps to make sure that you *never pay retail!*

3. Having a hunch, a strong intuition or a hot tip is only one piece of the puzzle. The Stock Report Card is one way of disciplining yourself to fill in the other pieces of the puzzle, including the competition.

7

THE SANTA RALLY AND OTHER WALL STREET SECRETS

Many of life's failures are people who did not realize how close they were to success when they gave up.
—THOMAS ALVA EDISON

There's a saying: "A rising tide lifts all ships." In 1999, you could have thrown a dart at a wall full of Internet stocks and come up with a winner. The same was true in 2003 (and many other preelection years, outside of 2007, which was sunk by the subprime mortgage mess.)

Historical trends are generally reliable but, like most everything else in life, not fool-proof. The expected (and charts and software boasting to capitalize on those trends) can surprise you with unpleasant events—like Hurricane Katrina, the subprime mortgage crisis and terrorism.

A low tide grounds all ships. It's very hard for most companies to swim upstream of a declining stock market. Few young technology companies, aside from Opsware and Google, survived the 2000–2002 Internet technology crash. eToys crashed and burned, as did many other brands that seemed destined to soar pre-Y2K, when we worried that malls would become a thing of the past. (Instead, malls became walking promenades—people became even *more* social.)

Though past performance is no guarantee of future behavior, there are a few factors that it pays to know about when you are determining whether or not to buy or sell, including:

CALENDAR TRENDS
- Santa Rally
- Back to School Stock Sales
- Summer Doldrums
- Preelection Year Rally

OTHER FACTORS
- Small Caps for Performance
- Large Caps for Stability
- Exchange-Traded Funds versus Mutual Funds
- Diversification and Asset Allocation
- Happy People Make Better Products Faster and Cheaper
- The Economics of Freedom
- Emerging Markets
- Historical Performance

CALENDAR TRENDS

Typically, 50 percent of the stock market gains each year are made within the last quarter of the year (which is how I made so much money in 2001, a year when most investors lost most of their money in Internet stocks). Preelection and election years have almost double the return of postelection years. Why not swim with the current? It's easier than trying to swim upstream.

The Santa Rally
Over 50 percent of the stock market gains each year are made in the last quarter, which is why Wall Street pros call the phenomenon the "Santa Rally." Knowing this may help you to determine your selling point. If you have a stock that has had a nice run entering into October,

you might want to wait until the end of December or mid-January to reap your harvest.

This is also why I suggest meeting with your financial partner in late January (historically the top-performing month of the year) to see if any stocks, funds or Exchange-Traded Funds in your nest egg have had a major run-up. This might be a time to lock in profits by selling some of your funds and rebalancing your portfolio according to your long-term life plan.

This alone could have saved you from the NASDAQ bust in 2000 *and* the real estate bust in 2006. (NASDAQ began its decline in March of 2000.) Both of those industries posted outstanding gains in the years before they busted out. Taking the profits and rediversifying according to your life plan would have protected you from having too much riding on those industries during the downturn.

Let's say you're thirty, and the markets have had such a great year that you now have 90 percent of your portfolio concentrated in stocks. At the same time, you think that legacy Blue Chips have seen too many days in the sun (and are overvalued). You can sell your "fading Blue Chip" ETFs and keep the money in the money markets or purchase another lower-risk, yielding investment, like bonds, in order to get the percentage back to 70 percent stocks with 30 percent safer. (If you did this with overvalued NASDAQ stocks in January of 2000, you were a genius because the dot-com balloon didn't start deflating until April of 2000!) So use a disciplined approach to asset allocation to beautify your bottom line.

There Are Exceptions to Every Rule

Now, as with just about everything else in life, there are exceptions to staying "all in" for the last quarter of the year. The Santa Rally trend didn't work for subprime mortgage investors in 2007. The subprime mortgage lender industry took a big hit in April, and by August the number of foreclosures in this market was increasing at a devastating rate. Even though many of the stocks in the subprime mortgage industry had lost most of their value in May, it was still a good idea to cut losses by selling as quickly as possible because it was easy to see that the wave of foreclosures from distressed borrowers was only beginning (regardless of what the lenders were trying to say about White Knights who were going to come in and save their companies).

Remember: When the income sinks overnight, that is going to be more than most companies can endure. It's the CEO's job to keep you invested, which is why they try to come up with all kinds of great arguments why their company is better than it looks. Those arguments might still be spilling out of their mouths even as they are meeting with bankruptcy specialists. New Century Financial bit the dust in April. Novastar Financial did a reverse stock split in July with every four shares of common stock exchanged for one share. (Reverse splits are a sign that a company is in great distress and trying to avoid a delisting of the stock.) Creditors began eating Novastar alive by January 2008.

So there are times, especially in your trading portfolio, when you ignore the Santa Rally and have to run with the changing dynamics of the industry.

How do you get the information you need when an entire industry becomes distressed? Here again is where it pays to have followed the rule about "invest in what you know" and have faith that you know more than you're giving yourself credit for. When an industry is distressed, the last thing you should do is to rely upon the corporation's communication to investors. It's their job to keep you calm while they struggle to correct the problem.

Savvy investors who cashed out of subprime would have simply checked to see the trend of foreclosures. Was it increasing? Was it likely to continue increasing? If so, wouldn't that continue to distress those companies that were left holding the empty bag on the loans, regardless of what kind of rah-rah speeches the mortgage lenders were chanting? The same held true for telecommunications before the wave of bankruptcies in 2002. Long distance prices hit rock bottom by 2001, and the competition was so fierce that there was little hope for increased earnings going forward.

Subprime mortgage lenders were just holding too much worthless paper to be valuable to a new buyer—regardless of what they were saying in their press releases.

Back-to-School Stock Sales

When's the best time to buy? September is historically the worst-performing month each year, which makes the back-to-school season a good time to stock up on stocks you've put on your shopping list. September comes right before the Santa Rally, so you have the wind at your back, most of the time, in most industries. For this reason, I suggest that your second meeting with your financial partner occur in late September—to search for Exchange-Traded Funds and index funds that you'd like to buy. (The prevailing theme, however, should be acting in line with your long-term plan.)

Now, again, winning on Wall Street is never a simple formula. You can't simply have a system that buys in September and sells in January. Remember the subprime story. But there is also another roadblock— the bewitching month of October.

Though October is typically a month with positive gains, October has also hosted some of the worst days in market history. Black Monday, October 19, 1987, was the day the markets shed almost 23 percent of their value. Black Thursday (October 24, 1929) and Black Tuesday (October 29, 1929) ushered in the Depression.

So you can see why it is not a good idea to rely upon market software that boasts of fool-proof returns. Not one of my colleagues trusts that there is any reliable system to the madness of crowds. And don't *fool* yourself—markets become overvalued because of the herd mentality, not because there is a shortage of real analysis and smart economists warning you of the consequences of jumping into the fire of an overheated industry or market. Unfortunately, most of the best and brightest economic brains are not the ones commenting on television, which is why I often refer my friends and subscribers directly to the blogs of certain Nobel Prize–winning economists, to the statistics agencies (like the Bureau of Economic Analysis and the Federal Reserve) and to the Investor pages of FINRA.org and SEC.gov.

Summer Doldrums

The summer months are reliably boring in the stock market, even in spectacular years like 1999 and 2003. Almost all Wall Street professionals take their vacations in August, which translates into lower volume, lower volatility and less professional attention paid to the markets. July is only slightly more active.

Sell in May and Go Away

Because stock market activity is going to slow down so much in the summer months, Wall Street pros say that you should "Sell in May and go away." This makes sense because the summer doldrums are just around the corner. However, in down years, you'll be happier that you took your profits earlier—in January—and in up years, there's not a lot of upside lost between February and April. (Remember, again, that you're not going to get too fancy with buying and selling in your nest egg, other than to rebalance your portfolio based upon a preset blueprint.)

Preelection Year Rally

The preelection years, like 1999 and 2003, are typically the top-performing year in the four-year election cycle. Odyssey Advisors CEO Paul Woods crunched the data for 164 years and 40 presidential elections and found that in the preelection and election years, the stock markets are more likely to provide double-digit returns, whereas in the two years after the election, single-digit returns are the norm. Preelection years serve up almost double the gains, on average, as postelection years.

PRESIDENTIAL ELECTION CYCLE—AVERAGE RETURNS
(BASED UPON TOTAL RETURNS, 1842–2006)

ELECTION YEAR	AVERAGE RETURNS, PERCENT
1 year before election	15.79
Election year	11.85
1 year after election	6.78
2 years after election	9.32

Preelection year 2007 started out with a bang and looked sure to follow that trend as late as October. Due to the pervasive economic implosion of the subprime lending crisis, however, the year ended up flat.

OTHER WALL STREET TRENDS

Small Caps for Performance
For your "Stocks on Steroids"—the trading portion of your portfolio—"hares" (smaller corporations with a smaller market value, a.k.a. capitalization) win the dash. Jabba the Hutt corporations (huge corporations, like Microsoft and General Electric) rule the universe but don't move much, so you don't typically see major gains in any one year. (The dividends are fun, however.) A good portion of the best performers featured in my e-zine were small caps, including

Google (at the IPO), Opsware, MySpace, World Water and Solar, and Taser International.

Large Caps for Stability

Companies that have been around for a long time and have a large market capitalization—over $10 billion—are great stabilizers for the long-term portion of your portfolio. The NASDAQ, where the majority of younger, smaller capitalization companies in the Internet-technology space were concentrated in 2000, lost over 65 percent of its value between 2000 and 2002. At the same time, the Dow Jones Industrial Average—which lists thirty of the large-cap "blue chips" like Boeing, Citigroup, Intel and Coca-Cola—went down only 22 percent at its lowest point.

These big, fat companies are not going to be making major run-ups in any one year, as a general rule, so don't expect them to supercharge your trading portfolio. Still, the companies with the biggest value on Wall Street typically gain 10 percent or more per year in share price value, which is well above the average annualized performance of all other assets, including real estate and gold. Besides, many of the large caps sweeten the deal for you by paying attractive dividends every quarter.

Exchange-Traded Funds versus Mutual Funds

If you've ever turned on a television, you've probably heard someone telling you to buy exchange-traded funds, or ETFs, which are merely a bundle of publicly-traded companies that are traded together as one single stock. ETFs and mutual funds are essentially the same thing in this regard. The difference between ETFs and mutual funds is that ETFs select their companies by using computers and preselected screens, instead of having a professional actively manage the fund (as mutual funds do). Since ETFs typically have a much lower cost structure, **pay lower commissions** and have lower fees attached to them than mutual funds, they're more popular with investors than they are with brokers. Many brokers rely upon the commissions paid to them by mutual fund companies for their bread and butter.

If you've found a great broker who is doing a bang-up job on your nest egg, it's hard to make a case for cutting their pay by insisting on ETFs instead of mutual funds. But for the "mass affluent" (as TD AMERITRADE Chairman Joe Moglia calls investors with under a million in their stock portfolio), who are really managing their nest egg themselves, ETFs have almost all of the benefits of mutual funds while being less expensive *and* part of a growing new trend on Wall Street (offering potential upside on the investment simply because others might buy in as well, pushing up the share price of your holdings). Online discount brokerages are more proactive about offering ETFs instead of mutual funds and many have designed a compensation plan that rewards their associates for assets under management instead of mutual fund sales.

ETFs, like the PowerShares Wilderhill Clean Energy Portfolio, had outstanding stock performance in 2007. WisdomTree ETFs have some of the most respected money managers on Wall Street creating their automated screens.

Diversification and Asset Allocation

Asset allocation simply means dividing up your investments among different kinds of asset classes, like stock, bonds, cash and real estate. (Money lent to your niece who's going to repay you tenfold when her Internet start-up goes public or her movie is snatched up for distribution is *charity* in my book.) Remember the golden rules: Always keep a percentage equal to your age *out* of stocks. Never be all in on any one asset class—not real estate, stocks, bonds, classic cars or your own business. (Your own business should be your income or hobby not your nest egg!)

Diversification is something that you do within an asset class. If you're amassing a real estate portfolio, you might diversify by owning an apartment building, office building and mall, in addition to your home. Or you could buy property in different cities (that you know something about). That way, if there is a hurricane in the South, you are not under water in the entire real estate portfolio (which is only a portion of your assets).

The same applies to stocks. Some years, clean energy is in favor. Other years, Internet stocks are going to soar. Metals were in the doldrums for decades before shining again in 2003 (during the worldwide construction and building boom). You diversify to experience the golden moments of an industry and to protect yourself from having the entire portfolio damaged by an area that loses its luster.

Happy People Make Better Products Faster and Cheaper

This is my personal economic theory by which I judge how well a corporation or a country is poised to perform in the future. Is a company attracting talented individuals who are on the ball, or do the salespeople look beaten up and worn down? You could have gone a long way with this in the airline industry between 2001 and 2005 when a number of airlines went bankrupt. It was very easy to tell which flight attendants and pilots were having fun on the job and which companies were struggling, experiencing more delays and working with disgruntled union members.

Happiness is directly tied to employee productivity, and you can tell how well this works by the number of companies that I've featured that go up in value. When employees are proud and excited to work for a company, they arrive on time, take pride in their work, increase their own productivity and tell their friends to buy the product. When labor disputes arise, workers walk off the job. And before the dispute gets to that level, the number of sick days increase, late arrivals become standard and the staff excels in whining, complaining, bickering and throwing wrenches into the works.

Remember it was my police officer cousin who first mentioned Taser to me. Police officers and politicians alike were looking for ways to avoid mortally wounding aggressive suspects. My cousin, like many police officers, was actually giddy about the ability to demobilize a suspect from 15 feet away using "less lethal force." As a result, command and training officers, like my cousin, were recommending that their departments purchase a Taser stun gun for every police officer in the force. City councils were finding the funds for these purchases. This was explosive growth waiting to happen—when easy payment options meet overwhelming demand. (Easy payment options + overwhelming demand are what fuel most boom cycles, including the subprime real estate boom/bust.)

You don't have to know the CEO to get some great scoop on a product or service that is poised to become in vogue. You know people who work in a lot of different companies and industries. Finding out what the morale is like in their workplace is easy. Who doesn't like talking about themselves?

My father commented to me some years ago that Kmart was in trouble, while most analysts were still giving the company a "buy" rating (and months before Kmart declared bankruptcy). How did my dad know? He went into the local Kmart store for some supplies he needed. The store didn't have it, and the employees didn't know when it would arrive. One of the clerks told him, "The shipments come in on Thursdays, but we hardly ever get what we ordered." He said, "You're better off going down the street to Wal-Mart." My dad took the advice, got his tool and then gave me the good counsel to avoid the stock!

The Economics of Freedom

This is a more sophisticated analysis about the underlying economic climate within a corporation or country that seeds the soil of pro-

ductivity. Rioting, labor strikes and war don't just happen unexpect-
edly. The economic growth of the company (or country) is apt to
wane or lag when the employees (or citizens) become distressed by
job loss or a decrease in salary and benefits basically whenever
people feel as though they're losing something. Productivity and
GDP boom when people feel that they have more freedom and
hope today than they had yesterday, even if yesterday was a period
of war.

We saw this struggle in many of the legacy corporations in the
United States between 2002 and 2007, when unions were fighting and
striking to save employee salaries and health benefits even while the
corporations were losing money. While the major American au-
tomakers were in heated negotiations with unions, the Japanese au-
tomakers flourished. Toyota became the number one automaker in
the world.

Western Europe began cutting back on liberal work and social policies in 2005–2006, and employees of some countries skipped work to
riot in the streets. Gross Domestic Product growth in those same
countries was anemic, whereas countries where citizens were excited
about their future (India, China and Eastern Europe) experienced incredible growth even though on paper, the citizens of India and China
were far "less free" than the Western Europeans.

Taking this to the extreme, it's pretty hard to make a widget in the
middle of a war—whether it's a war between unions and management or the kind occurring in Iraq and Myanmar in 2007. A worker
has less incentive to steal from or harm her neighbors when s/he
loves her job, is optimistic about her future and has more than s/he
needs. Some companies try to do the best they can for their employees (ask somebody about the quality of the food in their company
cafeteria and the policy toward flextime schedules), while others are a
real drag to work for. In the end, it's real people making the products—for better or worse for the company and the nation.

NATALIE'S NOTE

Corporations and countries that give their staff and citizens
more freedom and information to best manage their *own* future
have the competitive edge—not those corporations that hand
out defined-benefits plans (which are largely a thing of the past
these days).

Emerging Markets

When building and construction were booming in 2004, all of a sud-
den copper, a basic material in construction, tripled in price, after having been in a price rut for over a decade. The share price of major
copper mining companies like Phelps Dodge also tripled. Alternative
energy, as we've seen, was the top performer in 2007 after being in the
doldrums for three decades prior.

Emerging markets can be a new market, like social networking
(MySpace), or simply new blood in an old market, like corn, when
ethanol received so much government backing in 2007. If it's an older
company, you'll need to pay more attention to debt and the ability to
secure additional financing if needed at a reasonable rate. In a
younger company, you'll need to monitor cash on hand to make sure
that the company has sufficient funding to reach its goals.

Being aware of cash on hand and long-term debt is much easier
than it sounds and very important. Both line items are listed in the
earnings reports. I routinely "power search" the earnings reports that
are filed with the Securities and Exchange Commission, using key
words such as debt, cash, sales, income, revenue, liability, law suit,
management's discussion and disclaimer. I find that the most interesting information in the reports is centered around those words.
With the right keyword searches, you can easily turn up any skele-
tons in the closets, which might not be emphasized in the earnings
press release.

Historical Performance

Some stocks, like Microsoft, "trade around the core" of a certain price point for years and years. Over the first seven years of the new millennium, you could have bought Microsoft in the mid-twenties and sold it in the mid-thirties for consistent gains, over and over again, year after year. Other companies, particularly the younger ones, have a trend of increasing gains that plateau at a certain point. Still others, such as mega-corporations like Pepsico and Coca-Cola, trade in a steady range but provide great dividends. You can review the historical price performance charts easily on your favorite financial news site. It's just one click to create a one-, five- or ten-year chart. Very informative.

THE BOTTOM LINE

You can see now how buying low and selling high is easier said than done. We've just named twelve things to consider when you're making a guesstimate at which way the price is headed, and we haven't even tackled what most (underinformed) people believe is the fundamental aspect of buying low and selling high—price-to-earnings ratio.

NATALIE'S THREE TAKEAWAY TIPS

1. A rising tide lifts all ships, while a sinking tide can ground all ships. It's very hard for one company to go against the tide of the general stock market.
2. The majority of stock market gains are typically made in the last quarter of the year.
3. Smaller companies have more upside potential than the largest companies while big companies provide more stability and predictability for your portfolio than smaller companies.

PART 2

Get Involved

8

THE BILLIONAIRE GAME: HOW WOULD YOU LIVE IF YOU HAD ALL THE MONEY IN THE WORLD?

The more you praise and celebrate your life, the more there is in life to celebrate.

—Oprah Winfrey

"Retirement plan." Who picked a name that sounds about as inviting as a root canal for your most important budget line item? How about calling it your "Buy My Own Island Plan." Wouldn't you get a little more excited putting money into one of those?

When I divorced, my settlement was that my husband got all of the 401(k)—all the money we had—and I got to keep the condo, the one that was worth less than its mortgage. So I started out with no retirement plan at all. It wasn't that I hadn't thought about saving before. I, like so many others, always bought the diapers and the food and the toys first and found nothing left to invest. I never once thought that I'd be in a position to lose my home or to have to work full time; I always aspired to be a loving wife who shopped at sexy lingerie stores and an attentive soccer mom who picked up her kid from school and baked cupcakes for the team. But life doesn't always turn out as you plan. Which is why women especially need to set up their own nest egg—and do it now.

Here's a frightening statistic: 41 percent of single moms live at or below the poverty level. Single mothers are the largest group living in poverty; only 8 percent of married couples with kids under 18 live in poverty. So if you're married, a personal Buy My Own Island Plan, separate from your spouse's, is a great idea. None of these single moms, including me, ever dreamed that the fairy tale ends in poverty.

In the new fairy tale, husbands and wives have their own play and dream money. No matter how much you love and trust your husband, even if he is the breadwinner and you are the stay-at-home provider (with a thousand job titles), find a way to tithe to your Freedom Plan first, before the bills get paid, and stick to the Thrive Budget that I outline in this chapter *on your own*. There's no guarantee you'll get half of everything if you divorce. That's why you need to have your *own* dream blueprint and the money to help launch it.

THE THRIVE BUDGET (A.K.A. DOUBLE YOUR FUN BUDGET)

The basic breakdown of what I call a "Double Your Fun" budget is 50 percent to Thrive and 50 percent to Survive:

1. 10 percent to investing
2. 10 percent to charity
3. 10 percent to education
4. 20 percent spent on fun. (Half on immediate fun like movies, fashion and dinners out, the other half on something you'll have to save up for, like vacations, Jacuzzis, boats, etc.)
5. 50 percent for all your basic needs (including taxes, housing, food, clothing, etc.)

This budget places priority on living a rich life and investing there first *before* deciding on how much you'll spend on basic needs just to survive. Many successful entrepreneurs, artists and college students have an innate *knowing* about this Thrive budget, focusing more on education, investing, networking and fun than they do on basic needs. I've been incorporating it my entire life—having shared a home with five people during college to keep expenses down—and moving steadily up the income ladder of life as a result. Aspiring rock stars often pile into a sedan to promote their music across America—sleeping in the car as they travel between cities. Van Gogh focused on art, while his brother, Theo, covered living expenses. T. Harv Eker, in his *Secrets of the Millionaire Mind* book, and other self-help authors have discussed this strategy as well. The idea is not new. The focus is to *Thrive versus Survive*. Shift money that you pay on taxes (survival) over into charity and investing (thriving). Rethink the upgrade you did on your home as "fun" (so no more complaining that you don't take a vacation). It's largely a shift in thinking and focus combined with a blueprint to create a healthy, balanced relationship with abundant living.

Learning How to Thrive (Instead of Drowning in Basic Needs)
The idea of cutting out your café lattes and saving the two bucks a day is not a strategy for getting wealthy. That plan is all about deprivation and penny-pinching, is not going to get you out of debt *or* build your wealth, and completely sidelines the basic principle of real wealth— which is to step into dream-come-true living *now* (including those lattes and other pastimes that make you happy) by creating a better world, starting with your own life, then your neighborhood, then the world at large.

Living rich means valuing your life here and now, not waiting for sometime in the future when you can afford to be happy. Even if you're drinking cheap wine from a borrowed glass, even if your investment portfolio is so small that you have to save up for a few months to make your first trade, even if your 10 percent tithe is as small as a widow's mite, by investing in your future (through your investing and education funds), in your network of friends (through your charitable contributions) and in your health (through your fun), you are walking the path each and every day to the rich life (in every sense of the word).

Before you blow a gasket screaming about how unreasonable I'm being—your bills are too big and important to cut down so much!—let's consider why the biggest problem in your life isn't café lattes, it's the amount you spend just staying alive and all the complaining you do about your bills. Do you spend more than 50 percent of your income on your home, transportation, food, taxes, insurance and clothing? More than 70 percent? Are you trying to squeeze **all** of your Thrive budget—fun, investing, education and community—into less than 10 or 20 percent of your income?

Think about this on the billionaire level for a minute. (If you want to be rich, you're going to have to learn how to think as rich people think.) Bill Gates was worth about $58 billion in March 2008, according to *Forbes*. A 10 percent return on $58 billion is $5.8 billion annually. Let's call this his annual income. Do you think that he spends $2.9 billion on his basic needs? I'd venture to say that he's never spent anywhere close to 50 percent of his income on basic needs. Most entrepreneurs I know (including me) invest more in their business, education, charity and fun (also known as networking and socializing) than they spend on basic needs. Many sleep on couches and launch their businesses out of their parents' garage.

What did I do to cut my basic needs down to size? As a single mom, one of the first things I did was to find another single mom to live with. Instantly, my basic needs budget was cut in half, and my disposable income and free time increased dramatically. Incidentally, another very famous and powerful single mom did that—Gloria Allred (the famous attorney and women's advocate).

If you want to get ahead, forget about the pennies. Think about the big picture. Read on and I'll explain why charity is important, even if you think you're so poor you're the one who *needs* charity, and why

O.J. Simpson from living on the streets after the Goldman family won their $33.5 million wrongful death civil suit against him. Certain retirement plans cannot be levied.) Also, if you are investing right—in the markets but also in your education—you will actually get out of debt sooner than if you apportion a larger chunk out of your paycheck to pay down debt.

As your net worth and income increase, it becomes much easier to consolidate debt under more favorable terms and to increase the payments you make to pay it off. Let's take a windfall scenario where you inherit a million dollars. If you paid off $100,000 in debt first, your principal is reduced to $900,000 overnight. If you invested the money, then your debt could be paid with the first year's returns, as average stock market returns are over 10 percent annually, which is over $100,000. So, within a year you could pay down the entire debt and keep your $1,000,000 principal intact.

Don't worry about having to know everything about which IRA or 401(k) is right for you. This is what the brokerage houses were made for. The brokers are supposed to be up-to-date on all the latest capital gains taxes, tax-protected accounts, etc. Tax laws and qualified accounts change year to year, so by the time this book is printed, what is available to you could have increased yet again! In 2008, there were IRAs, 401(k)s, SEP IRAs, Roth IRAs, Health Savings Accounts, college funds, trusts, Annuities, insurance plans, endowments and more to choose from; your broker should be savvy enough to help you determine which plan is right for your specific needs. For additional guidance, check out FINRA.org.

2. Tithe to charity

The next 10 percent of your take-home pay should go to a charitable organization. Get creative! Tithe to the nonprofit organizations that you really want to support, not just your church. In many cases, your contribution is tax deductible, so you are actually decreasing the amount you pay to taxes here as well! You're learning how to "thrive" with the first 20 percent of your income, simply by shifting money away from taxes into tax-deductible vehicles that happen to beautify your own future and our world.

Why is charity so important? Because here is where you'll find your passions and your people. Consider getting actively involved so that you can start networking/partnering with people who have the same interests as you do. Partnering with people who share similar passions is a great way to enrich your life *and* your business prospects. Step up and volunteer for positions that will stretch your skills. Don't just take the easiest job.

Everyone asks me how I went from English major and part-time teacher to vice president in my first business job without doing the typical climb up the corporate ladder. My answer is charity. Immediately upon graduating from the University of Southern California, I volunteered my time as the chairperson of the silent auction at my son's elementary school. It was a high-profile public school in Santa Monica, and the woman who mentored me in the position was a very high-profile business leader in the state of California. Her business skills and her rolodex were both impeccable. The first year (before I graduated), I volunteered to solicit for silent auction donations. The following year, when no one stepped up to chair the event, I threw my hat in the ring. (In charity work, oftentimes the one with the most important job is simply the person who commits to doing it without being paid.)

While I was teaching, I also wrote (and won) grants for an underserved public school to implement an arts program that had been proven to increase academic performance. (The kids actually adored learning!) Those skills—as an executive managing hundreds of volunteers and processing over $50,000 in retail items in *one* day, as well as writing and winning grants—were invaluable! Even though I wasn't getting paid and was donating my time, I was increasing my own value, my skills, my achievements and the pay and the position that I could earn at any job in the future. So instead of spending *years* climbing the corporate ladder, I spent one year in the nonprofit world and jumped right to the top of the game.

Through the connections you make by tithing your time and money to charity, you will automatically begin attracting a new type of person into your life. As an unexpected benefit, the executive directors of organizations I have donated to have become a part of my circle of friends, my advisory board, and have invited me to hang out with some of their VIP friends, even though I was donating on a fairly modest level. You'll also notice that the spiritual director of the sanctuary I attend (and donate to) wrote the Foreword to this book. Supporting an organization doesn't guarantee you that level of endorsement—you'll need to earn that respect over time—but it does ensure that you'll be hanging out with the right crowd that is accomplishing great things. Those qualities rub off, just as much as if you were spending your time in a bar and drinking in the qualities of that atmosphere.

Charity can also be quite fun. As just one example, the American Airlines Ambassador Program (www.airlineamb.org) allows you to get on board with other humanitarians to bring care and compassion around the world. While doing good, you'll bond with others and add power and weight to your network of people. How's that for a different type of vacation. (Combining budget funds from fun and charity is allowed for an excursion like this.)

3. Tithe to your education fund

The next 10 percent of your take-home pay should go to an education fund. Education is your key to a better job and higher pay. The more education you have, the greater your earning power for your entire working life. Doctors make more than gardeners; chief exccutive officers earn more than dishwashers. Car mechanics who work

on today's computerized engines make more than mechanics who re-
pair the old gas guzzlers. As your education level goes up, so does
your intellectual capital and your salary.

Continuing education also provides opportunities to meet and
bond with peers. I met most of my most important business colleagues through educational conferences—from the Milken Global
Conference in Beverly Hills, to the Human Forum in Costa Rica, to
the Peace Alliance Conference in Washington, D.C.

Getting educated, getting a better job and staying abreast of cutting-
edge applications within your industry are the easiest ways to improve
your quality of life—to rush you from the world of hand-to-mouth
and into the world of "Hmmm. . . . what should I do with all this left-
over money?" Whether you're a teacher who's taking credits to get her
master's degree (and a raise), a manager taking classes on weekends toward an MBA (and a raise), a pediatrician who's learning more about
investing (to earn money while you sleep) or a CEO speaking on a
panel with your competitors, your bottom line will improve as you
learn, master and employ your newfound skills.

As Oprah said when she developed her Leadership Academy in
South Africa, "Education is the key to unlocking the world, a passport
to freedom." Never stop learning.

4. The Fun Funds

Fun is an investment in endorphins, which is a free "happy pill" and
one of the best health remedies you can drink in. Studies show that
enjoying life reduces stress and lowers blood pressure, which means
less money spent on doctors. Again, shifting to Thrive from Survive
doesn't have to cost more—it's about getting better returns. Health is
wealth, translating into fewer prescriptions, lower insurance premi-
ums and lower doctor bills. Fun is health.

Whether your idea of fun is yoga, surfing or a nature walk, exercise lowers your blood pressure and increases your blood flow, which
increases your productivity and earning potential. Lack of health is

one of the surest ways to encounter the most serious money challenges anyone will ever face—reduced income combined with strangling medical costs.

When you consider the credit card debt in the United States, it is easy to see that fun is a budget line item that is way out of whack. Shopoholics, like alcoholics and bulimics, are not having fun when they binge. They *overspend* to stop feeling bad or sad (because spending more never takes away the pain) and then have extreme regret later on when they have to face a mountain of debt (at a high interest rate).

I actually take 10 percent for my immediate fun budget in cash and spend it until it's gone. That's more enjoyable to me than counting receipts. Some of my favorite fun things are yoga, spinning, movies, dinner, massages and facials, as well as slightly bigger splurges like a beautiful silk blouse, a nice bottle of champagne or maybe a new Skype phone. If I run out of short-term cash, then I have to wait until my next income check to buy what I desire.

The other 10 percent goes for bigger adventures—a trip to Bali, original artwork, that huge flat screen television or a Jacuzzi. When you think that 20 percent of your workday is spent just for short-term and long-term fun like this, imagine how much more you'll enjoy your work! And when you enjoy your work more, imagine how much more you'll *put into* your work. And that kind of investment in doing a better job could easily mean more income or a raise and a promotion. When you get excited about living, that energy infuses potential and positive results into everything that you come into contact with—including your investments.

Now some people say, "I enjoy my house. That is my adventure." To which I reply, "Great! So stop complaining that you never go on vacation." You can also think of this portion of the budget as "no whiners allowed." I'm not telling you how to define your fun. I'm simply telling you to appreciate it, to get creative, to stick to the proportions and to really delight and bask in the experiences you choose for your free time. Focus on creating and enjoying the life you desire instead of drowning in the life you dread.

5. Basic Needs

Only half of your take-home pay should go to basic needs. All of them—from taxes to food, housing, clothing and debt repayments. When you're a billionaire, you'll have more going to taxes, security, staff and other expenses than to your home, and when you're a thousand-aire, you'll have more going to the home and less to taxes, so this allocation works on both sides of the scale.

My friends and subscribers almost stop liking me when I get to this part of the plan. Their faces scrunch up, and they want to scream in protest!

Yes, it's going to require making big, bold choices with regard to your earning potential and dramatic cuts to your expenses—for now. Did you really think that pinching pennies was the solution you were looking for? Have any of your other get-rich schemes actually worked?

If you want a better life, the solution is rather easy but hard to implement if you are used to whining and complaining that you never have enough money. Quite simply, you have to increase your income and decrease your spending. And, at least in the beginning, this will be uncomfortable because it is a big shift away from your old way and everything society tells you to do—at least through the ads on television. But, ultimately, because you are investing in fun today and in your dreams and your future, you'll have a much more enjoyable life almost immediately. Your kids might enjoy you more if you downsize to a new solar-powered, sustainable home with modest square footage than the energy hog McMansion where everyone hides in their own dorm room. Instead of whining that you don't take vacations, you might start hosting monthly potluck yoga parties at your beautiful home (as a friend of mine does) and enjoy your home more, as part of your "fun."

If you're working at a job you hate in order to afford mortgage payments that leave you so squeezed each month that you and your spouse scream at one another on date nights, no amount of therapy is really going to get your life back into balance. You can try to be nicer and love one another more, but every waking moment is still a crisis waiting to erupt. Loving and being lovable is key to great companionship, but you also need an action plan to remove the major stress factors as well. Money is one of the things that breaks up marriages. Get it in balance and watch your relationship improve.

Are you living in a huge home that sucks up more energy than the state of Rhode Island? Do you really need to live in a home that big? Are you paying thousands of dollars for your mother or father to live in their own home when they could live in the guesthouse out back for free or in a less-expensive senior community, where they would be enjoying life even more? Are you a single mother who could cut her expenses in half and have her paycheck go twice as far if you moved in with another single mother, sharing expenses, childcare and household duties?

This is why the house-sharing premise behind CoAbode.org—one of the most effective springboards for struggling single mothers—is also useful for elderly parents, college students and aspiring rock stars. When people share basic chores as well as expenses, there's more time and money for the fun . . . instead of work, work, work, chores, chores, chores, homework, bills, crying, hair pulling, arguments, sadness, resentment. . . . Remember *The Odd Couple*, the vintage film and television series about two divorced men who share an apartment? They were as ill-matched as two people could be, but they still made it work. Get creative.

I drive a nine-year-old car. It's a beautiful German car that runs very well, gets great gas mileage, and the fact that I'm still driving it means that it's not polluting a landfill somewhere. I love driving my beautiful car, and very few people know that it is as old as it is because it looks expensive. It feels almost like a member of the family.

Driving a car that's too expensive for your budget or living in a house or apartment you can't really afford is not doing you any good if it makes you an unhappy, overburdened person who screams at your loved ones every time they spill milk on the hardwood floor or leave the door open, running up the heating or air-conditioning bill. Having a budget that allows you fun, investing, philanthropy and education plunges you immediately into the person you always wanted to be. By having a plan for tomorrow, which includes enjoying today, you get to experience "the rich life" moment to moment—both in dollars and in smiles. Freedom is not a zip code or a car model. Every soul has her own sanctuary geography. It's simply living in a way that makes your spirit sing.

You will be amazed at how quickly balancing your lifestyle and budget, and contributing regularly to your investment portfolio, translates into measurable gains. And you'll also be amazed at how your relationships improve when you're happy with the choices you make and are actively creating a life that's valuable and enjoyable every single day.

Creating the Life of Your Dreams

The Thrive Budget is not just for the middle class and the working class. I have two girlfriends who are both multimillionaires. I have often found myself in their kitchens listening to their worries and concerns about money—even when I was in danger of losing my home (and, yes, I put aside my own concerns long enough to have a cup of tea and listen to theirs). One was concerned that her husband was sucking the equity out of their multimillion-dollar real estate holdings to keep a Dead On Arrival business on life support. The other had an independent film she was producing that was turning out to be more of a tax write-off than a viable blockbuster.

Of course, odds are good that the film producer will still be in her home fifty years from now (trust fund) and the income property owner will never be out on the street. But, in the short term, those money pressures *felt* life-shattering and caused severe health problems in both families. The Thrive Budget doesn't fix everything, but it provides a structure upon which every financial decision is a balanced part of a larger vision and game plan—which you design throughout the playing of the Billionaire Game.

This Billionaire Game is an exercise that plumbs the depths of your soul for your purpose for living. How you would live if you had all the money in the world? That life plan becomes your blueprint for where you should be investing your time and money (on a smaller scale) today—in order to *create* the life of your dreams.

For instance, if the film producer thought of her film as charity—and it could have been because it was a film with a strong social message—she would have rested more easily at night, regardless of the profit potential. (She could benefit from the tax write-off after all, and she was bringing an important message to light in an entertaining way.)

If the Thrive Budget were in place in the income property owner's household, her husband wouldn't have permission to tap the home's equity for a losing business proposition. (The Buy My Own Island plan is not a bank!) He'd have to find viable capital solutions for his business elsewhere.

Young or old, rich or poor, have a vision, healthy money habits and your own personal freedom plan. You can start now on your own, regardless of how healthy or unhealthy your partner's money habits are.

GET RICH AND ENRICH

Wonder how I could listen to the money woes of my multimillionaire friends when my own situation was dire? Sometimes, I was literally scraping change out of the bottom of the couch for dinner. Why didn't I ask for money? Because I was safe, healthy, happy and had a plan to create the life of my dreams. Besides, I was grateful to both of these women, who, in their own important way, helped my son and me survive the tough times, sharing things we needed at key moments, whether it was a ride home from school or a Sunday dinner.

They were an integral part of the "Mom Network," which any single mother needs to survive. And they were my friends and had been, through thick and thin, for a long time. I was as concerned about their overall health and happiness as they were for my livelihood.

When things are tough, you must hold hard and fast to grace and dignity. It's not always easy, of course. But begging, whining and complaining do not add any beauty to that picture. And, I had enormous faith that the Thrive Budget was going to kick in and work, and I didn't want to ruin the experience by annoying everyone around me.

I had confidence that I could transform my life by adhering religiously to *the flow of money*. That meant that even if I had $10 coming in that week, $1 went to my investment plan, $1 to charity, $2 for fun, $1 for education and only $5 for basic needs. Sure, I had to get creative with making that work. There were dozens of shareholders in my first company, most of who received a percentage of the company for providing services essential to the business. My attorney provided legal counsel and set up the corporation. My home office was paid for with shares of the company instead of cash. I am completely blown away that my part-time (independent contractor) graphic designer continued to do amazing work—taking units in the LLC instead of cash—during periods when we simply did not have the income to pay him.

So, there was one night when I slept in my car (and my son slept with his father) so that we could continue operating. (My friends came through with interim housing after that one night in the car.) There were many days when one-dollar burgers were the main food being consumed and many nights when we were elated to be invited to dinner at someone's home! (You'll recall that most dot-coms went bankrupt between 2000 and 2002. I launched in 2002, when there was literally no money being invested in online businesses!)

And yet, my son and I always managed to have fun—continuing our tradition of weekly family nights, of singing "I love you" in the mornings to each other and of listening to loud music on the way to school. (Neither of us are morning people, so the music was more fun than trying to grunt at each other.)

I'm not saying there were never times when the stress didn't overwhelm me. In the beginning, I paid my monthly bills on the nights my son was with his father so that I could spend half of the night biting my bloody nails, wringing my hair and lighting bills on fire without getting committed to a mental institution. However, over time and with a solid plan, my son and I learned to enjoy each day (even if he didn't own all the toys his friends had), to create a new life and to envision an awesome future.

One year, in fact, there weren't **any gifts** at all at Christmas. I wrapped a few things that were really lame—hand-me-down items that I shouldn't have even bothered wrapping and a couple of really stupid gifts from the dollar store—hoping that having something to unwrap was better than having no gifts under the tree. Of course, my son was hoping for a video game console, so my 10 percent fun budget of a cap gun, sports cards and the silver peace ring that I had been wearing for the last decade was about as pleasurable as coal in the stocking. After a few long moments of extreme disappointment, marked by powder keg explosions in his incredulous eyes, my son shoved all of the gifts back to my side of the couch. He allowed himself to be hugged and begrudgingly said that he loved me, too.

I laughed (with a few tears in my eyes) and said that we'd probably look back at this Christmas as one of our favorites because we were still hugging and smiling (I was; he wasn't) even as we opened the worst gifts anyone on the planet had ever received. Those moments sting, but the soul-enriching that occurs when you face adversity—the realization that no gifts at all brought two people closer than any *thing* ever could—is priceless. I would *never* have had the courage to *create* that Christmas lesson for my son, and I'm not saying that I was a happy participant when the situation was thrust upon me, but as I look upon the young man today, I know his soul is more beautiful as a result.

While I would have wanted only the best for my son, including pots of money and a family that didn't break up, he learned that our home was built on love, even when there weren't elaborate gifts exchanged on holidays. And since that time, all of his gifts and our living environment have steadily improved.

THE BILLIONAIRE GAME

How would you live if you had all of the money in the world? Below is a game that will help you get started dreaming of your billionaire lifestyle right now and discover how you would live if money wasn't an issue any more.

In order to really shake out the old and invite in the new way of thinking about life, I want you to fantasize about what the Thrive Budget could mean for you where you are now, then if you were a multimillionaire, then as a billionaire. You'll be following the Thrive Budget, but you will be spending more and more money in each category until you are spending just like a billionaire.

It's just a game, but watch what issues come up for you.

Starting with the income you are earning right now, add details to each of the categories of the Thrive Budget, beginning with investing and ending with basic needs. To which specific organizations are your charitable donations going to go? Which companies are you buying in your stock portfolio? What kind of housing are you building and moving into—a green, solar energy-efficient house? Will you buy a bike to save on gasoline costs? Will you manage your own stocks and bonds or hire a money manager? Where will you go on vacation this year?

The first column is for your initial year, starting now, but the second column is what you'd be spending if you earned $1.2 million annually (not your spouse—this is *your money*). For some of you, this is Fantasyland—something to aspire to—so knock down your walls and fences and go for it. This is time for outrageous, vivid, detailed, "dream come true" planning. It is the same you—but with a much bigger monthly salary!

The other columns are designed to get you thinking wayyyyy beyond your current income and lifestyle. Imagine you're earning a take-home salary of $100 million per month. How will you invest that? Where will you donate ten million dollars this month? What kind of immediate pleasure can you have with that kind of money? What kind of "long-term fun" splurge will you buy with $120 million (twelve months times $10 million per month)?

When you get to the basic needs in the final billionaire column, remember that you're spending 10 percent on charity and 10 percent on education, both of which could be tax deductible.

	First year (YOUR SALARY)	$100,000/month (Millionaire Status)	$1,000,000/month (Multimillionaire Status)	$100 Million/ month (Billionaire Status)
10 percent: Buy My Own Island Investing Portfolio				
10 percent: Charitable Giving				
10 percent: Education				
10 percent: Short-term Fun				
10 percent: Long-term Fun				
50 percent: Basic Needs Debt consolidation House Car Taxes Food Clothes				

PLAY THE BILLIONAIRE GAME

What came up for you? Did you have difficulty spending $10 million on charity? Or on pleasure? Did you actually curse me when it came to some of these categories, as if it were ridiculous to imagine spending such an outlandish amount of money?

Ahhhh . . . But this is the life of a billionaire. It's not just about having a beautiful family, expensive cars, magnificent jewelry and a huge home that magically cleans itself. There is a tremendous amount of responsibility involved. In fact, security may be a part of your basic needs. There will be a professional money manager handling your investments. You'll have a staff to maintain, a business to run and employees to provide for. When you become a billionaire, it is more like being royalty. You have to imagine yourself at the center of a large estate with people on your payroll, investments and orchards to fertilize, harvest and maintain. When you think of education, you'll be considering the benefits to the community of having neighbors and employees with a higher skill set, not just your own increased brain power.

Some people find it very easy to spend $120 million on long-term fun (your own island or a theme park, a la Walt Disney's Disneyland). Others wouldn't dream of that kind of narcissism and could only imagine a long-term fun budget of $120 million each year that benefited the rest of humanity (launching a Shakespeare in the Park series all across the Southwest, sponsoring summer camps for underprivileged youth, putting playgrounds into underfunded urban elementary schools.).

What many people come to realize through this exercise is that money is not happiness. Money becomes a responsibility. It doesn't matter how big and beautiful your home is, if the neighborhood outside is at war, and, conversely, if there are big beautiful parks in the city, like Central Park in Manhattan, people can live in smaller spaces and still feel happy. Most people can't come close to spending $100 million a month on pleasure . . . until they include other people. And then, magically, it becomes easy.

A side benefit of this exercise is that it shatters old (and largely untrue) myths about being a wealthy business owner. When you see money as abundance—like a farmer sharing more fruit than s/he can eat with her neighbors—you can love the idea of making money by investing and becoming rich. You have a plan that is well-balanced, which keeps you honest and humble without being self-sacrificing. Americans as individuals are the most giving humans on the planet. Many of us are no longer stuck in survival mode and are able to share our abundance with other humans around the globe. These are the gifts of prosperity—a world that works for all.

But the truly most important aspect of this exercise is that you uncover the true you—who you would be and how you would act if you had all of the money in the world. There is no reason why you can't start activating that vision now. If you hate war, then refuse to invest in mutual funds that invest in defense companies. If you hate cigarettes and cancer, stop investing in Altria (which is Philip Morris's tobacco company). Put your money where your heart is and watch the world become more beautiful as a result.

THE BOTTOM LINE

We live in a time when single mums can be richer than queens and an immigrant can be one of the richest people in America, like Sergey Brin, the cofounder of Google. J. K. Rowling was able to dream up an entire universe around Hogwarts, complete with Quiddich and He Who Must Not Be Named. She is now richer than the Queen of England. Your dream life should be as rich.

NATALIE'S THREE TAKEAWAY TIPS

1. How would you live if you had all of the money in the world? You can unlock that passion, have that vision for yourself and start walking that path right here and now.

2. The road to prosperity means that you are focused on thriving—on your investments (the first check you write), your charities (which lead you to a new network of friends), your education (which increases your income) and your fun (health is wealth).

3. Basic needs, including housing, car, gas, insurance, taxes, debt repayment, credit card bills, etc. should not exceed 50 percent of your income. Oftentimes, writing checks for education and investments means you write a smaller check to the IRS. Not more money, just a different allocation and a different way of thinking.

9

BROKERS ARE SALESPERSONS, NOT SURGEONS

In a genuine relationship, there is an outward flow of open, alert attention toward the other person in which there is no wanting whatsoever.
—ECKHART TOLLE, AUTHOR OF *A New Earth*

Walk into a brokerage. Who is that person greeting you at the counter with a hopeful smile, anxious to sign you up as a customer? S/he would like you to think of him/her as a master of the markets, but in fact, brokers are salespersons, not geniuses.

Stockbrokers have one of the hardest jobs and the highest turnovers of any profession. Becoming a licensed stockbroker does not require a college degree. In fact, it doesn't even require that the person ever attended any college at all. And, most of the time, the person greeting newcomers at the counter is very low on the totem pole.

So, you're going in expecting the person who greets you to be an expert on investing when in fact s/he may not have ever made a dime in the stock market. Brokers—whether they sell mortgages or real estate or stocks or sailboats—are paid on commission, not on having a winning record or making money for their clients. (Money managers, on the other hand, are experienced brokers who can demand a minimum investment and take a percentage of the gains—something available to you, once you're a millionaire.) In 2007, the headlines were screaming about unscrupulous mortgage brokers who had taken advantage of unsuspecting subprime borrowers; during the

2000–2002 recession, the ones sporting targets on the back of their jackets were the stockbrokers.

This is why it's so important to interview this partner as if your life depended on it—because your life*style* does. Your choice of a life companion is the single most important decision you'll ever make, and the choice of who handles your money is the second-most important. (Because you don't get to pick your parents and kids!)

The smart, wise, experienced broker that you want to have on your team has come to understand that acting in a client's best interest is the best payoff over time . . . but her success has earned her an office of her own with a closed door. S/he has few, if any, shifts at the front counter. For many of the frontline brokers, on the other hand, the job they find themselves in isn't what they dreamed about doing when they were in kindergarten, and it won't hold their interest for long if it doesn't make them rich quickly. That's why you'll probably see a new face at the counter frequently, with an especially high turnover during recessions. So when you go looking for a broker, your first challenge will be to identify who is in the job for just a few months and who is building a lasting career in the financial services industry.

One of the first questions that you should ask is simply, "How much should I put in the stock market?" You now know that you should keep a percent equal to your age safe. If the person before you says "as much as you can stand," or "most of it," and you're over the age of 39, then you should just say, "Thank you," and leave. If the broker begins with a percentage close to what's appropriate, then you can proceed with some of the other questions that I've listed below.

Many investors approach the task of finding a financial professional much as they do finding a job, thinking they have to sell themselves to win the relationship. Instead, you should be treating the broker as you would a fiancée. Don't sell yourself. Make sure s/he is worthy of you. Dig into her past. Ask the hard questions. Your life, your needs, your risk tolerance and your areas of expertise are specific to you, and if any financial professional starts laying out a cookie-cutter plan for your money, that's the first warning sign that you're dealing with a salesman instead of a professional who's looking to develop a mutually beneficial long-term relationship.

DETAILS, DETAILS, DETAILS

Now, if your broker starts getting huffy about answering your questions, that is your sign to be even more adamant about getting them answered— especially if s/he starts spouting off that old, worn-out line that "You wouldn't operate on yourself, so why are you trying to manage

---

TWELVE QUESTIONS TO ASK YOUR BROKER

1. How much of my portfolio should be in stocks?
2. What tax-free accounts should I consider?
3. How many years have you been in the business?
4. What is your education (including university and financial services)?
5. What financial certifications do you hold?
6. Are you a value or a growth lover?
7. What is your research criteria—i.e., analyst recommendations, news, earnings reports, NataliePace.com's Stock Report Card . . .?
8. How many clients do you currently service?
9. What is the performance of your clients' portfolios?
10. How many years have you been with your current company, and where did you work before?
11. Have you ever had any complaints filed with FINRA?
12. How many market downturns have you personally worked through?

---

your own money?" Someone who is in it for a long-term relationship, built on trust and integrity, will understand that you want to make the best choice possible. Someone who is in it to make as many commissions as possible is the one who will resort to hard-sell tactics. Below are clues to the kinds of answers your dream partner will be giving you.

1. How much of my portfolio should be in stocks?

This is the most important question you can ask a potential financial planner because it gives you a reliable gauge of whether or not the person in front of you is more of a saint than a salesman. Experienced financial professionals are familiar with the basic tenets of Modern Portfolio Theory.

The premise of this theory is that as you age, less and less of your portfolio should be invested in the stock market and more should be allocated toward safer, steady-yielding investments. As a person's reliance on their portfolio for income turns acute, their ability to stomach risk diminishes. If retirement is just around the corner and the person in front of you is trying to convince you, for any reason, that you should have more than 30 percent of your nest egg in the stock market, you should move on to Candidate B immediately. You don't even need to continue with your questions. You are dealing with an unscrupulous broker who is in it for the commissions, not for your best interests. If you are twenty, it's not going to be hard for the broker to give you the right answer on this question, but listen carefully to the rationale s/he employs.

Mutual funds are stocks. Exchange-traded funds and index funds are stocks. Bond funds are stocks. Individual companies are stocks. "Safe" investments include bonds (not bond funds), certificates of deposit, money market accounts and treasury bills.

2. What tax-free accounts should I consider?

Creating tax-free accounts is the single most important job of any great financial planner, outside of maximizing return on investment.

Your portfolio will compound at an exponentially greater rate if you are trading within a qualified, tax-free retirement account than if you have to pay capital gains on every sale. There are all kinds of great options for tax-free accounts, and your broker is supposed to be well-versed and up to date with recent legislative proposals and changes. Be sure to ask about all of the maximum individual retirement contributions that you qualify for, as well as college savings plans, health savings accounts, trusts, foundations (if you are a high-net-worth individual) and others. This single consideration could increase the bottom line of your assets by many times over the course of the decades.

3. How many years have you been in the business?

You don't want to babysit a newbie. If the person is still wet behind the ears, let her learn on someone else's money! Five years of experience—minimum—is a good benchmark because that increases the likelihood that this person has been through a market downturn and survived well enough to keep her clients happy.

4. What is your education (including university and financial services)?

If you're sitting in front of a rock-star broker or an actor broker or a rodeo rider who just became a broker, s/he needs to have hit home runs on the preceding questions for you to invest the time in asking any more. Otherwise, you can cut the date short and reward yourself with a grande latte and a yoga class. You deserve it for being smart enough not to hire a fool to sit in the king's chair of your portfolio.

5. What financial certifications do you hold?

Nothing but the best financial certifications should be behind the second most important life-partner decision you'll ever make. If your portfolio is worth less than $250,000, chances are you're not going to get a Charter Financial Analyst helping you out, so be realistic, but also be choosey. At minimum, you want to deal with a Certified Financial Planner, and her certification must be up to date.

6. Are you a value or a growth lover?

What is the broker's investment style? If you like risk and return and your broker loves value and stability, this may not be a personality match. The lackluster gains may be too boring for you to endure. Likewise, if you've got an adrenalin junkie in front of you who is making your stomach queasy just listening to her describe the rush s/he gets from investing, that could be a deal breaker, even if s/he's answered every question right on the money. Money is such an emotional subject that a mismatch on investment styles with your broker could be bad for your health. You can get adventure on a vacation. Ideally, your relationship with your broker should be rational, predictable, calm and always proceed according to a carefully constructed plan.

7. What is your research criteria?

Any broker you're considering who relies solely on "what the company tells us to pitch" could be more driven by company sales incentives than real gains in your portfolio. You need to know, though, that most brokerages limit what their staff can recommend because the company doesn't want any young-gun brokers shooting off recommendations from the hip, which is a free ride to Lawsuit City. Whether it's technical analysis, a favorite guru, analyst recommendations, my Stock Report Cards or earnings reports, you should have a clue about what is motivating the broker to pick up the phone and call you and be able to trust that it isn't simply because s/he's short on commissions this month.

8. How many clients do you currently service?

This question is for both you and the broker you're considering. It will give you a realistic view of how much your broker is thinking of you when you're not in her face, and it will give the broker a nudge that you are aware of the fact that s/he has a lot of people competing for her time. If the response is ridiculously low, then you're dealing with someone who'll say anything to win your business. If the response is honest, then you should inquire as to how s/he organizes her time to bring quality attention to the masses while still keeping everyone happy about the bottom line. The average broker at a low-cost brokerage has a client base of over 400. (Yes, it's virtually impossible to provide personalized service to that many clients!)

9. What is the performance of your clients' portfolios?

Be careful that you don't get a bait and switch on this one, where they point you to mutual fund pie charts that have been carefully selected to present a positive picture. If the charts end more than six months ago, that's a red flag. If the broker offers some excuse about why s/he isn't able to provide both short- and long-term data, that's another. If they give you a return that looks amazingly high, ask if it is a "cumulative" return. Cumulative returns must be divided by the number of years to come up with the average return every year. Also ask for the annualized number.

10. How many years have you been with your current company and where did you work before?

Note particularly how long the person has been in the financial field and what industry s/he was in previously. Ordinary common sense applies here: Longer-term employment equals greater stability. If the broker has switched brokerages once or twice to maximize career potential or for a promotion and raise, that's a good sign . . . provided she doesn't have a graveyard of past employers, which may spell trouble.

11. Have you ever had any complaints filed with FINRA?

You can check out the truth of the broker's story with FINRA.org, where complaints against brokers are logged. Note that if this is a new broker, s/he may not have had enough time in the industry for the clients to become disgruntled with the way their nest egg is handled.

Don't use a clean FINRA report as the sole measure of a great broker. Do take note of any concerns.

12. How many market downturns have you personally worked through?

Don't confuse a bull market with wisdom. Anyone could have made great money picking stocks in 1999 and 2003. Returns in the years in between were harder won. If the broker started in the business at the end of the last recession, s/he has really only seen good times and might not know how to make it through the more challenging years.

WHAT TO DO WITH THIS LIST

Is it okay to go into a brokerage office with these questions written down, as if you were interviewing a job applicant? Of course. Interviewing job applicants is exactly what you're doing. In fact, you should be interviewing at least three broker candidates, just as you would if you were dating to find the perfect life companion. Brokers and lovers—it pays to pick a good one! You want and deserve a broker who will communicate with you in plain, easy-to-understand English and who will make you feel comfortable when explaining her recommendations and decisions.

So bring the list of questions, ask them all, and while you listen carefully to the answers, also pay close attention to his or her attitude.

EIGHT QUESTIONS YOUR BROKER SHOULD BE ASKING *YOU*

In addition to the questions you ask your broker, there are also a number of things the broker should want to know about you. If s/he doesn't ask questions along the lines of the following, you have to expect that this person will be offering you cookie-cutter solutions instead of what's best for you.

1. What is your risk tolerance? (No investment is worth having a heart attack over. Most brokerages have a few questions that determine this.)
2. How old are you?
3. When do you want to retire?
4. How much money do you want to have when you retire?
5. How much can you afford to add to your investment fund each month? (10 percent of your take-home, right!)
6. Do you have any 401(k)s or other pension plans and annuities that you would like to roll over? Are you sure that you haven't forgotten any at an old employer?
7. Do you have any special tax considerations?
8. Would you benefit from a Health Savings Account, a SEP-IRA or a college fund?

You want the financial planner you choose to be someone you can respect, admire and honor through thick and thin. If not, you're setting yourself up for losses, because at the first sign of real trouble, you'll be faced with the hard truth that you knew all along—it was a bad match to begin with. You don't want to be stuck in the foxhole with a jerk, a novice or a self-interested mercenary.

You want and deserve an experienced professional who will be an ally, holding your hand and guiding you through the hard times and celebrating success in the good times. All markets—real estate, bonds and stocks—have their rallies and their pullbacks. Investing, like life, isn't a fairy tale, but if you pick an outstanding partner, it can be a rich and rewarding adventure.

CHECKING OUT YOUR CURRENT BROKER

If you want to check up on a broker or Certified Financial Planner that you're already doing business with, simply look at your brokerage statement. If everything you have invested is in stocks or funds (of any kind, mutual funds, ETFs, index funds or bond funds), no matter what your age is, you should start interviewing new brokers immediately.

If, on the other hand, you have a percentage of your portfolio equal to your age that is *not* invested in stocks or mutual funds, that's a sign that your financial planner might be experienced wise and looking out for your best interests. (In doing this evaluation, count bonds and money markets on the "safe" side of the ledger, but not *bond funds*. Bond funds are simply a grouping of bonds that are traded like stocks, and thus, are subject to the same risks as other stocks that are traded. Additionally, unlike bonds, bond funds never mature.)

If your broker passes this asset allocation test, then you can begin having more faith that you are with someone who has the skills, expertise and experience to do a good job for you. (I'd still recommend going through the list of questions with your broker and possibly interviewing other possible candidates, especially if you've only known your broker for a brief period of time—just to be sure that you've made the best possible choice.)

If your broker fails this test, the next step is to start interviewing other candidates and to contact FINRA to see if the broker has any complaints on file. If s/he has been overly aggressive with your portfolio, s/he may already have a few complaints on file from other disgruntled clients. A visit to the BrokerCheck listings at FINRA.org or a call to them at 800–289–9999 will let you find out if there have been complaints.

CYBER-BROKERS: MISSING THE GREED CHIP

There's no substitute for a great Certified Financial Planner. S/he can truly be a wonderful asset, help you navigate tax considerations, present retirement plan options, help you outline and achieve your financial goals and perhaps even play a role in educating you to be more market savvy.

However, if you're new to the investing game, it will pay to be ultra-safe while you learn enough to interview and identify a reputable Certified Financial Planner. It's very difficult for brokerage houses to monitor self-interested brokers (until after they're sued by a slew of unhappy clients), so even the most reputable brokerage firms are vulnerable to the unethical actions of any one associate.

Since the birth of Internet brokerage firms, investors have had another alternative. If you're comfortable using the Internet, you can open an account with an online brokerage and establish a diversified retirement plan in under fifteen minutes. Doing it yourself will save you money on commissions and give you more control. Since a cyber-portfolio that you manage yourself is not subject to the whims and greed of commission-motivated brokers, this is a viable option, especially for young, newbie investors with a smaller portfolio who are comfortable trading online. (Remember that people with under $100,000 in their stock portfolio very often land with a broker who has little more experience than her clients and is handling hundreds of other accounts. On the other hand, if you have over a million dollars, you qualify for active money management from some of the most reputable individuals around.)

The online discount brokers offer the same types of Individual Retirement Accounts, 401(k)s, college funds, health savings accounts and more as the full-service brokerages do. By answering a few questions, you can set up your portfolio and, in some cases, have the plan rebalance according to a preset, personalized formula. Note that in many cases you are able to roll over your existing retirement plan or 401(k) into a new brokerage with no penalty. You may qualify for the rollover, even if you're still at the company, if the company makes any changes to the plan during an election period. If you do roll over to a brokerage, you will have significantly more choices on the stocks, funds, bonds and money markets than you do in the company 401(k). A broker can easily identify if you qualify and assist you with the details of the rollover. (Yes, most online brokerages also have brick-and-mortar offices and customer service call centers to assist you.)

Hmmm . . . I never thought I'd think a computer was the best partner, but in this case, the online discount brokerages may have found the first solution for America's newest challenge—protecting the individual investor who must now navigate Wall Street on her own. Many of these portfolio software programs are based on Modern Portfolio Theory and clearly help you determine your risk tolerance and time line. Think of these self-directed retirement plans as a way to practice your dating skills while you get educated enough to interview and hire the dream certified financial partner for a long-term relationship.

NATALIE'S NOTE

If you click on a brokerage that demands personal information from you before you can try out their products, just log out. There are plenty of online brokers that allow you to test-drive their products without providing any personal information.

THE BOTTOM LINE

Did you ever hear Warren Buffett talk about the billions he made by listening to his broker? No. His broker was probably screaming mad in the late 1990s when Warren refused to jump into technology. But

Warren Buffett only invests in things that he knows and understands. And he's one of the richest men in the world as a result. Your broker is there to advise and coach, but you're a better partner if you are strong and wise, assured of what your long-term goals are and promoting investments that you are behind in heart, mind and soul. At the end of the day, it's your money and your loss, if the investments are not handled right. So, be sure that you know your partner well and that s/he is worthy of your trust and faith.

NATALIE'S THREE TAKEAWAY TIPS

1. Brokers are salesmen, not surgeons. Many brokers push the funds that their company tells them to and/or the ones that they earn the most commission on.
2. FINRA.org is an online resource where you can find out if there have been any complaints filed against your broker candidate.
3. Brokers who are just starting out can have over 400 clients to service in order to make a living. Interview the broker as if your life depends upon it because your life*style* does.

10

INVESTMENT CLUBS: FRIENDS' NIGHT OUT WITH BENEFITS

The more you include others, the more smoothly things flow and the more easily things come to you.
—ECKHART TOLLE, AUTHOR OF *A New Earth*

In 2000, when I got serious about investing in stocks, it was a lot like going out on a blind date. I had plenty of raw data, lots of information, but no idea what it all added up to. One peek at the date candidate gives you a pretty good idea whether or not you want to go forward, but how do you peek into corporations? And, as anyone who has ever been on a blind date knows, information can be very misleading. "He's got a great personality" usually means he's uglier than the Hunchback of Notre Dame. "She's very smart" is a wink-wink way of telling you she's a bookworm, not a supermodel.

How do you know which stock to buy or home to purchase when the person who's supposed to be advising you on your decision is earning her bacon by selling you something?

I had an abiding distrust of the stock market (and blind dates). Wasn't it just legalized gambling? Weren't corporations inherently corrupt? If the odds were against a novice investor like me making a profit, and I assumed they were, why waste even one spot of time on it?

Instead of surrounding myself with cats and eating ice cream out of the container, I turned to something that humans have used to their advantage over the long road from cave dwellers to condo dwellers: I turned to my community of friends. It struck me that some of them had started companies that were very successful. One of them in particular, Ben Horowitz, was launching a company called LoudCloud with Marc Andreessen, and I knew him to be a pretty nice guy. (We used to hang out when he was in college, eating Oki Dog on Hollywood Boulevard—pretty yucky, but it was affordable. Ben was the brother of my boyfriend, Jonathan, back in the days when I was a singer-songwriter.) It began to sink in that maybe there were other honorable CEOs out there, too.

As I thought about it, I realized my circle of friends included people who could give me a hand in other ways, as well. I've always been on very friendly terms with numbers, but you'll rarely find me shopping for anything. So even though I now had some tools and a network to help me determine more about the CEO of a company I might be interested in, I often didn't have a clue about some of the most basic products and why anyone liked this thing more than that thing. My friend Brigitte, on the other hand, loves shopping and hates math. Len understands market terminology. Jonathan serves on a lot of board of directors. Patti enjoys the thrill of penny stocks and has information on the most obscure companies you've ever heard of. Diane is decades deep in real estate experience. Vicki, cars. Carol, entertainment. And so on.

If we could find a way to distill the collective experience of our friends and acquaintances into usable information, then we'd have a far more complete picture of the companies whose stock we were interested in buying. In fact, if one could line up all of the publicly available data and information and then factor in our own consumer experience, wouldn't that put an individual investor at a significant advantage in making informed investment decisions? Shoppers have access to all sorts of proprietary information that is completely legal because it comes from their own observations, and when you share your insights with friends, you can get a pretty good sense of whether some new trend is catching on with the general public.

Guys have their poker games, their Monday night football or golf with their buddies. Women have girls' night out, Bunko, Mah Jong or book clubs. But let's face it, there's hardly an endorphin more thrilling than money, unless perhaps it's chocolate, and the last time I checked, chocolate won't power your private jet (although I'm thrilled that it's now an important part of our daily diet!).

So Brigitte, Patti, Diane and I, along with several others, formed an investment club of soccer moms in January 2002. That year proved to be one bear of a test. At the October 2002 low, NASDAQ was down 75 percent from its March 2000 high. The Dow dipped over 15 percent that year. Most investors were ready to throw in the towel. The husbands of my girlfriends used to walk in on our meetings and say, "Don't you girls read the news? This is a crappy time to start an investment club." They were thinking that our portfolio was off as badly as the markets were—but they were wrong.

We were actually making money—not a lot, not as much as we wanted, but enough to give us hope. Of course, at the time, since we were just beginning, we had no way of knowing what would come, but my friends trusted me when I said that October 2002 might well be the market low, that there were economic signs that 2003 would be a much more delightful year and to ignore the headlines (and their husbands). And in the meantime, our monthly dues were only $100 each, with the added benefit of all that fun and social time we were sharing.

In 2003, when the markets turned around and our investment club began enjoying some real outstanding gains, the women were very excited to be doing so well *and* learning how to invest at the same time. When I cashed out my portion of the club in April 2004, the club and I had doubled my investment—and launched a new company, The Women's Investment Network, LLC.

Imagine how the tune of the hubbies changed—from doomsday warnings to gleeful interruptions—when our account had more than doubled. No matter whose house we were in, the husband always found an excuse—delivering glasses of wine, making sure we'd had enough dessert—to peek over our shoulders to see what companies we were considering that month. It's so much fun to see a giddy husband with plates of cake and glasses of wine in his hand!

The 100 percent gains that I enjoyed in less than two years with a group of soccer moms made me proud of our achievements and thrilled with our gains. It doesn't get much better than that. Especially when you consider how close our friendships got over the years, how many delicious meals we shared and how each woman learned to tithe regularly to her own Buy My Own Island Fund and to invest that money wisely so that it worked twice as hard on her behalf. One of the women went on to have six digits in her private investment account. A few years later, she started a new club where the buy-in was $10,000.

The Women's Investment Network, LLC, an online financial news, information and education service, targeting women, endured a number of years of cash-negative operations before the glorious success that we expect to enjoy as a result of this book. Most of our competitors, as well as the majority of online businesses launched in 2002, weren't as successful.

It's your choice just how ambitious you and your friends wish to be, but, at minimum, why not enjoy time with your friends while at the same time pooling your brains and money for greater gains? Whether you have an all-girls' club (a girls' night out with benefits), or a couples' club with returns, or a mixed singles' monthly soiree, the tips below will help you maximize your gains and your enjoyment. I mention all of these variations on how your club might be set up because, in my view, the more fun you make it for the members, the more you'll remain committed to the monthly meetings and invested in the collective outcome. The social and the education aspects are as important as the money. Use the wisdom you learn in your club to fuel your own investments.

When you pool your money and partner up on the research, the power of your dollar goes a lot further eight or ten times as fast. (It's not very cost effective to buy $100 worth of stocks when $8 or more is going for trading fees; it's much more sensible to have $800 to invest in one selection each month.) Also, the peer pressure on each member to write a check for the dues every month means that it *gets done*. If you've been waiting to have enough money to invest, chances are your cash flow is out of whack and you're stuck in the rut of basic needs, trying to scrape together pennies for fun, vacations and annual IRA contributions *after* everything else is paid for. Once you get religious and routine about investing and see the monthly check you write to the club as another one of the basic bills—which is usually what happens for all the members—your nest egg grows on autopilot every single month. (And with the power of returns, it can really grow quickly, as ours did.)

If you're worried that the research demands will be too much, rest easy! The research task is typically handled by a different member each month, so you might only be stuck doing research once a year. And, of course, you can apply all that you learn in the investment club to your own larger, personal portfolio. As a group, you'll be defining exactly how you want your research presented, what companies and sectors you'll be interested in and what your monthly dues are. Below are some tips to help you get started.

THE SIX STEPS FOR STARTING AN INVESTMENT CLUB

1. Recruit members
2. Form a limited partnership
3. Create a members' agreement
4. Set the dues
5. Provide for taxes
6. Establish responsibilities for the officers

Recruit Members

The goal of an investment club is to have low overhead and low operating maintenance so that you can maximize returns. If you find a small group of friends whom you really like socializing with, the odds that you'll have a satisfying, successful experience are increased exponentially. If you start bringing in friends of friends whom you hardly know and have never broken bread with, the odds increase that the situation will get more complicated.

Why? Because money is one of the most emotional aspects of life. Money is the primary cause of the destruction of marriages, so imagine what can happen to your little partnership if you have seven or so people focused on getting rich and one penny-pincher in the crowd. Or, vice versa; if you have a club of penny-pinching accountant-types, one freewheeling entrepreneur might add too much spice to the mix.

Here's what I recommend you do before you start recruiting members. Find a couple of people you really admire and respect who are enthusiastic about the idea of an investment club; you and they will become the core group. Then ask each one of them to recommend one or two people whom they really admire and respect. Before you officially add anyone to the group, have a meal together out on the town. Watch how everyone interacts throughout the meal and especially when the bill arrives.

Did someone get sloppy drunk and blather on nonstop about war and traffic or the environment and politics? Who forgot to add tax and tip when they threw in their money for the meal? Who suggested that the group should shortchange the waitress because s/he didn't show up fast enough with the pepper? Who tried to skip out without paying? These are all telltale signs of how a person interacts with money. Be sure that you don't ignore them.

A friend of mine tells me that his hiring criteria is based on what he calls his three-hour theory. Never hire anyone you wouldn't want to sit next to on a three-hour plane ride. In this case, never recruit anyone for your investment club you wouldn't want to enjoy a meal with. (Typical investment club meetings start with dinner at six-ish, followed by the meeting.)

It's far better to have fewer people in the group who really like and trust one another than it is to add someone who's going to be trouble down the road. Let the temperament and vision of the core group provide the road map for your recruiting. When 4 Times Square—the world's first green skyscraper—was conceived, the developers—the Durst Organization—didn't recruit the guy who designed the Leaning Tower of Pisa or hire a foreman who showed up late every day. Be picky.

How many members should be in your club? It depends on your desires, but in my experience, part of the returns of the club is social. It's a lot easier to make everyone feel as if they have a voice if everyone has a seat at the same table. For our club, ten (which we started with) felt too large. Eight proved to be the magic number.

Form a Limited Partnership

I met a woman at a conference recently who had been in an investment club that had recently disbanded. "Why?" I asked.

"The corporate taxes killed us," she answered.

An investment club of friends should not be set up (and taxed) like a corporation. Corporations are set up when people have employees and are conducting business. Investment clubs are not doing business and have no employees. They are nonprofit partnerships, and partnerships are not subject to the same mandatory taxes that corporations are. (In California, the minimum tax to run a *corporation* is $800 a year, which can kill your returns in the early stages of the club. There should be no minimum taxes in most cases to run your investment club, other than the taxes you'll pay on capital gains.) That woman's investment club disbanded and lost money because they didn't set it up correctly.

This falls into the "check with your accountant first" category. Tax laws change all the time, and this is one area that you have to get right from the outset, before you start operating.

You'll most likely end up with a limited partnership, so gains are taxed to each member at their personal tax rate instead of the group being taxed at the corporate rate. The Internal Revenue Service in the United States and the Canada Revenue Agency both make it very easy for limited partnerships that are nonprofit (not doing business) to get a Tax Identification Number (in Canada, a Business Number) over the phone *free of charge*. Check their web sites for the information that you need and then make the call.

You will need this tax identification number when you set up your investment club account at your brokerage. By the way, there is no need to take out one of those "doing business as" (DBA) newspaper ads, because you will not be doing business. So, even though you should have a clever name for your investment club to distinguish yours from other clubs at the brokerage, don't waste the money publishing your name in the local press—unless you come up with a name that is *so* awesome you think you might want to use it for business later on. (And in that case, you might consult a trademark attorney to register the trademark, as well.)

Create a Members' Agreement

This is key: You don't want to set up your investment club without having all of the members agree to all of the terms of the club. You might think that you're all friends so you don't need this, but when it comes to money, it's very important that everyone understands exactly the way that the dues are handled, who gets to vote on the stocks you buy and sell, what happens when someone doesn't pay their dues and so on. When all of these issues are handled and the policies are spelled out beforehand, you just read the agreement like a Bible when issues arise, instead of having long, heated discussions trying to solve them. The member agreement really is your club rule book, and just like any game, when the rules are clear, everybody can focus on the fun.

A member agreement spells out the operating procedures of many contingencies, like:
- How much are the monthly dues?
- What happens if a club member wants to drop out?
- Should different requirements apply in the case of a family emergency or if a member has to move away?
- What happens if a club member dies?
- What happens if a club member doesn't pay her dues?
- What percentage of the club members must agree before a trade is made?
- What officers will you have and who will fill the posts?
- What will be the responsibilities of each officer?

With a Member Agreement, the idea is to make sure that most of the likely sticky situations have already been addressed and few things have to be debated after the fact. This makes transitions easy. If someone can't pay their dues, there's a road map for what happens, which is a strong incentive for everyone to pay on time and stay committed to the group.

There's no need to start writing a Member Agreement from scratch. Sample agreements are available on the web from various sources. You can download the template and plug in the values that are right for your group. One source is my own site, NataliePace.com, where a sample agreement is available as part of the "Investment Club Startup Kit." This kit is offered free to purchasers of this book; just go to NataliePace.com and click on the Investment Club Startup Kit banner ad to download the kit.

Before passing the new document around for signatures, you'll want to have it reviewed by an attorney.

Set the Dues

Dues: Hmmm . . . How much would you feel comfortable spending on an evening out? That's a good start. You want to make sure that the dues are set at a rate that the members can easily afford each month without feeling overburdened (and without causing an argument with their partners).

For you and anyone else in the group following my Thrive Budget, the dues could be a portion of your tithe to your investment fund. The bulk of your 10 percent monthly contribution to your nest egg should be going into your own account with a long-term, diversified strategy, and not subject to the vote of anyone other than yourself, with the input of your certified financial partner. Alternatively, at least a portion of the investment club dues could be considered as part of your education fund.

Provide for Taxes

A capital gains tax applies when you sell a stock. Again, tax laws change, so be sure to check with your accountant to find out how much of your profits to set aside for taxes each year. Typically, stocks that you buy and sell within a year (considered short-term capital gains) are taxed at a higher rate than stocks that you hold for longer than a year (long-term capital gains).

The club will have to pay an accountant every year to review the books and prepare the tax return. You'll want to select an accountant, find out what the charge will be and hold enough money aside so that when tax time comes you can pay that expense. Fortunately, tax time occurs after the Santa Rally, when it is typically a selling season rather than buying season. You might even consider having December or January dues partially set aside for taxes. (Remember to set aside taxes on your capital gains, in addition to the fees associated with preparing the return.)

You'll need to file a tax return every year. Make sure the return is filed on time: Late filings are punished at a very high rate in the

United States, which can be up to $50 per member per month. A return has to be filed even in the early years when you might not be selling any stock or posting any capital gains.

Establish Responsibilities for the Officers

Your club cannot hire employees (otherwise, you're in business and may be taxed differently) so the members have to divvy up the responsibilities among themselves. Here again, it's your club, so you get to pick who does what, for how long and when you'll rotate responsibilities. However, the following guidelines should be helpful in determining the best person for each job.

Treasurer

In an investment club, the treasurer is the most important job, so be sure to pick the most responsible member of your group and make sure that person has superior skills in math. The treasurer should be the person with the responsibility for placing the trades with the broker, as well as working with the accountant to make sure the taxes get filed on time.

Most investment clubs are only buying one stock a month, so this job shouldn't be too time intensive. Reports should be made each month to the club, but again, most brokerages offer easy online portfolio access, so copies can be printed out for each member, with the only time spent being one click to print the document. It's not hard or time-consuming, but these tasks are essential. Your club will fall apart without a strong treasurer, which is why I list this job first—before the president.

President

While all of the club members will be listed on the investment club brokerage account, there will typically be only two member "agents" who have access to withdrawing funds or writing checks on the investment club account. Since your club won't be writing many checks (mainly to the accountant and to any member dropping out), it's a good idea to have two signatures required for checks and withdrawals.

The president should also be responsible for making sure that the account information remains accurate with the brokerage and the IRS and that the affairs of the club run smoothly. For this reason, I would list the president's name and address as the primary agent with the Internal Revenue Service and with the brokerage, while also making sure that the treasurer is able to access the same information and make trades easily online.

Vice President

The vice president is often in charge of setting up special education nights. Consider that education is a part of the mission of many investment clubs and that you should have one or two meetings a year devoted to getting smarter about investing. Your local brokerage might offer a course on online trading or a day-long conference. There might also be a money manager who would come to speak to your group. Be sure to find someone who has been in the business for several years—preferably at least seven. And, as mentioned earlier, consult "BrokerCheck" on the web site of the brokerage industry trade association (FINRA.org) to make sure the broker has no complaints on file. The educational evening should feature an expert, not a salesperson.

Secretary

It's very important that the meetings are well documented. At a minimum, the secretary should keep notes on who attended the meeting, who paid dues, what stocks were considered and which stock the group decided to buy shares in. Minutes from the prior meeting should be distributed and accepted at each meeting. Also, it's extremely important that the secretary logs the buy/sell date and price of each trade. I've made it easy for you to keep track of that information in an Excel spreadsheet, which is available with the Investment

Club Startup Kit online at NataliePace.com, under the Investment Club Startup Kit banner ad.

Duties for the Researcher of the Month

Your club will find its own way with regard to research. There's no set way that will work for every club, though it's very useful if the research person completes a Stock Report Card to be distributed at the meeting. The Stock Report Card lines up the key facts of the company under consideration *and* its competitors. (You can find a blank Stock Report Card template on the home page at NataliePace.com under the "Investor Edu" section.)

Each member may have her own unique style for presenting companies and data, which I think works better than dictating a standard style that may not be comfortable for some. If you meet at a place with a computer, you can always go online and get some more data for consideration before the vote on whether to invest is taken. Try to have options for getting more information if needed—even if it means sending a husband scurrying to the Internet—so that the member who did all the work that month doesn't get criticized by someone else who thinks some crucial piece of information has been left out. And remember, you can always table the vote until the following month, after the additional questions have been answered. (Try to avoid making anyone feel like a dope; the goal is education, empowerment and gains.)

At the end of each meeting, you'll discuss and agree on a market sector for the next meeting and find out who might have an edge in that particular industry. If you're interested in clothing designers, is there a person in the group who is in the fashion or retail industry? If you're interested in solar energy providers, does anyone have solar panels on their home? Make a list of companies that your club might be interested in, or leave it up to the member who takes on the task of bringing the research to the next meeting.

THE BOTTOM LINE

An investment club is a great way to have a monthly night out with friends—with benefits that can last a lifetime. Since you're investing only a small amount each month, don't get over-analytical, over-critical or over-technical. It's your club, and you and the other members will find the ways of handling matters that works best as your club grows and develops. And remember: You can apply what you learn in the group to your own investments and in that way have complete control over the portfolio that really matters—your own.

NATALIE'S THREE TAKEAWAY TIPS

1. Investment clubs work better if the members are people who know and like one another and have similar approaches to money.
2. Make sure that you set up a limited partnership and register with your tax agency as a not-for-profit entity. You're not considered a business because you do not have employees and are just investing with your friends for fun and mutual gain! If you set up your club as a corporation, many states have high annual corporate taxes that could potentially wipe out your gains or even have you operating at a loss.
3. You must file your tax returns on time. The penalty for filing late in the United States is $50 per partner, per month. Imagine how horrible that is and how fast that penalty multiples!

11

SOCIALLY CONSCIOUS INVESTING

The Warrior of the Light projects his thoughts beyond the horizon. He knows that if he does not do anything for the world, no one else will. So he fights the Good Fight and he helps others, even though he does not quite understand why.
—Paulo Coelho, author of *The Warrior of the Light*

According to the Social Investment Forum, $2.3 trillion (out of $24.4 trillion under professional management) was traded with socially conscious criteria in the United States in 2005—*nearly one out of every ten dollars*. Socially conscious companies embody open and transparent business practices, ethical values, respect for employees, communities and the environment and have a vision of working for the world at large, as well as shareholders. Whew! Quantum physics might be easier than figuring out which companies are socially conscious! Who has the time? Fortunately, there are a lot of watchdog organizations that make the job easier than it sounds. And, thankfully, there are a number of socially conscious mutual funds available, which can exponentially cut down your research time.

In 2007, the best-known socially conscious funds were Domini and Calvert. I'd love to report that being socially conscious was good for your wallet, but over a ten-year period, those funds underperformed. Ouch—not what those socially conscious visionaries of the late 1990s hoped would happen.

CLEAN ENERGY EARNED ALMOST 60 CENTS
ON THE DOLLAR IN 2007

But their vision might still come true. The happy news is that the top performing industry in 2007 was alternative energy, after being virtually nonexistent for the prior three decades. With the explosion of interest in alternative energy and green investing, a number of additional socially conscious mutual funds and ETFs have begun to sprout and more will likely follow. Green was so hot when I was writing this book that I had to keep updating this chapter. Al Gore won the Nobel Peace Prize. Oil hit $100 a barrel, but investors still loved the clean energy stocks more.

There will be a slew of brokers and friends who are anxious to warn you that this approach was a loser in the past. Remind them that driving while looking in the rearview mirror is a good way to crash. The Internet was a colossal loser for investors from 2000–2002 before Google went on to become the most successful IPO of all time. Apple Computer single-handedly resurrected the music business at a time when the music companies were trying to sue their customers into paying for downloads and Tower Records had to shut its doors. Don't be stuck in the past, ever.

Just to illustrate how hot companies are becoming when they take the socially conscious high road, consider one of the top performing stock picks in 2007: World Water & Solar. I featured the company in my April 2007 ezine. Just one month later, in late May, the company's chairman and CEO, Quentin T. Kelly, traveled to Toronto and Vancouver with California Governor Arnold Schwarzenegger on the California Trade Mission to Canada. Mr. Kelly was selected due to World Water & Solar's leading role in building prominent solar energy projects in California, including the Fresno airport solar complex and the largest solar-powered agricultural system in the world, as well as the only self-sustaining water utility. World Water & Solar was also selected to provide ten solar-driven water-purification units for use in Darfur, Sudan, that will each deliver some 30,000 gallons of safe drinking water daily at sites throughout that ravaged desert region. This is the kind of company that thrills the socially conscious investor and the capitalist alike.

I bring up this company as an example in particular because World Water & Solar was trading off the boards during that time period—meaning that if you had been pouring over technical charts or earnings reports or analyst recommendations, you would almost certainly not come across this one. The company was not a holding in any mutual fund. The only way you could have stumbled on what a player World Water was becoming was by looking at the products, the customers and the forward-thinking projects that the CEO was engaged in—by investing in the company as an individual stock.

Additionally, as the ultra high-risk investment, World Water would typically be the first stock dumped in a panic if there was any concern in the larger stock markets. So what happened when the subprime mortgage market stumbled so badly in the summer of 2007? Instead of plunging, World Water came through strong, while the blue chip stocks took a beating. The stock markets look like a flat line by comparison to the stellar returns that World Water posted and sustained during the period between April, when my feature article on the company appeared, and September, when Chairman Bernanke and the Federal Open Market Committee cut the fed funds rate by 50 basis points in an attempt to restore confidence in the capital and credit markets.

Investors who take positions in these green, socially conscious companies are less willing to give them up—even in uncertain times. In that case, new investors are going to have to pay a higher price—something we all love when we've bought our positions early.

MAKE LOVE WITH YOUR MONEY

Interested in socially conscious investing but want to try a newer fund? WisdomTree, iShares, PowerShares and the American Stock Exchange web site all list ETFs, grouped by industry, investment style and other factors of interest. (Yes, absolutely, industries like clean energy and natural health cures can be considered socially conscious.) Doing a search for socially conscious mutual funds or ETFs on your favorite engine should also yield results. Calvert and Domini have web sites. Also, it's your broker's job to know what funds are out there, so s/he should be helpful in your search as well.

Even if you don't want to become an activist investor, what you might not realize is that chances are *very high* that you are already invested in all kinds of corporations that you may not wish to support. If you have a retirement plan at all—whether it's a 401(k), annuity, IRA or pension plan—you are invested in mutual funds, and each mutual fund invests in hundreds of publicly traded companies.

Every wonder how Philip Morris could make it through those decades of lawsuits by the cancer victims? With *your* money. Ever wonder how Exxon Mobil remains the largest corporation in the world with a market value of $500 billion (in January 2008)? With *your* money.

I meet people all the time who hate smoking but invest in cigarette companies because the dividends are so strong. Others complain about a "war for oil" in Iraq but drive gas guzzlers and have oil company stock (some without knowing it). In September 2007, Altria (Philip Morris) was one of the top holdings in the four most widely held mutual funds. Exxon Mobil was the largest publicly traded company on Wall Street. Translation: If you own a mutual fund, chances are you own Philip Morris tobacco company, Exxon Mobil and all kinds of other companies and activities that you may not want to support—whether you are anti-oil or just sick of watching a tanned Larry Ellison (CEO of Oracle) buy Malibu real estate and race sailboats.

Is there really any reason to invest in clean energy over oil, defense and tobacco companies? Well, yes, even if the sole reason is that you want to participate in the world's top performing industry (in 2007, and likely going forward as well). Why not invest in the products and services that are cleaning up our world? If Al Gore is right that global warming is a life-or-death concern, investing in clean energy could save our planet. If he's wrong, we end up with cleaner air, land, water and energy. Sounds like a win-win to me.

There are a lot of naysayers out there who pshaw the idea that you should engage your desires and emotions at all in investing, to which I reply, "Good luck." Emotions are the criminals most responsible for stealing your gains. Like it or not, when your stocks go down in value, your blood pressure boils and you want to dump them quickly, and when they rocket up in value, the shock and thrill keep you clinging for dear life, even when it's a good idea to let go. In other words, your emotions are your own worst enemy when you are invested in things you don't really like and have no idea how to value. Your emotions can be a great ally when you are invested in things that are enriching the world, and you are confident that those investments will continue increasing in value in the years to come.

Seeing what companies your mutual funds are invested in is as easy as two clicks on your computer. Literally. That easy. On any major financial site, you can simply enter the 5-letter stock symbol of the mutual funds you currently own, then click on "Top 25 Holdings" to see what companies you're supporting.

If you don't like what you discover, then simply tell your broker that you want to own funds that are more socially conscious. There are index funds, exchange-traded funds and tons of easy options for you to choose from that target companies more in your sweet spot. Or, you could create your own socially conscious nest egg with a basket of carefully diversified stocks, with the help of a professional. It's not that hard, and a good broker will be a valuable asset in this.

Once you get these holdings set up and tucked in properly, you just keep feeding the portfolio with your regular monthly deposits and check up on it twice a year.

THE BOTTOM LINE

I'm really glad that I don't have to ride my horse to New York City, so I'm grateful for the role that oil and gas played (in the past) in making our lives easier. I'm just confident that if we can walk on the moon, we can invent solar-powered planes. (We already have solar-powered space stations.) If we can end slavery, we can end poverty. If we can eradicate polio, then we can find a cure for cancer that is better than chemotherapy. Collectively, our money promotes and creates the products, goods and services in our world. Like it or not, whether you know about it or not, U.S. corporations use *your* money to decorate our home here on planet Earth.

NATALIE'S THREE TAKEAWAY TIPS

1. Most people have no idea what they are invested in. If you have a pension or a 401(k) and you don't know what you own, chances are that you are an owner in the status quo—big oil, big tobacco companies, big defense companies, et al.
2. Clean energy was the top performing industry on Wall Street in 2007—earning almost 60 cents on the dollar. Energy (oil) came in second at 32 cents on the dollar.
3. When you realize that our world looks the way it does on your dime, you can start investing in (and reaping the financial and global gains of) products for a new, cleaner world.

PART 3

Get Savvy

12

THE HARE WINS THE DASH; JABBA THE HUTT RULES THE UNIVERSE

Companies with the smallest market capitalizations produce the highest returns. As companies get bigger, returns go down until you get to the blue chips, which produce the lowest returns of all.
—PAUL WOODS, CEO AND PRESIDENT, ODYSSEY ADVISORS

Everyone knows the mantra "Never pay retail," but it's a lot easier to apply that to shoes and ties than it is to stocks. You may feel so completely flabbergasted with numbers that you'll never understand the stock market enough to determine whether it's poised to go up or down. You might have taken a painful hit with Internet stocks between 2000–2002 and fear jumping in to experience a sequel. And yes, there are some periods when the stock market (or the real estate market or the bond market) is simply overvalued (too expensive) to go all in at once. But, trust me, you can really do this.

Since the U.S. stock market has that beautiful historic return of 12.4 percent every year for the past twenty-five years, as of January 2008 (see Figure 12.1), if you are stuck with something that has gone out of style, you can just store your stocks (in your long-term portfolio) in the back of the closet without "wearing" them. Just like shoes, chances are that in a few years, what you're storing will be all the rage again, and you'll be glad that you didn't junk them (this holds true with bonds and real estate as well). Quality products and services hold up over time and increase in value—provided you didn't pay an outlandish price to begin with for them. And if you are keeping a percent equal to your age safe and are diversifying your assets, you've really got an investment insurance plan, with very little trouble at all.

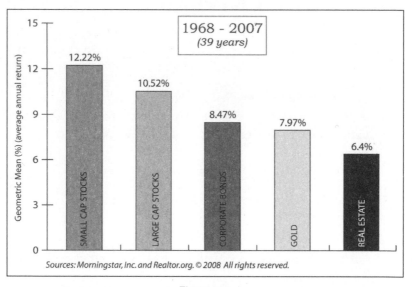

Figure 12.1

Some people think that having an understanding of average price-to-earnings ratio for the general marketplace can be very helpful, but when you're just starting out, this data can actually be more confusing because there is not a clear correlation between low P/Es and bull years (when the stock market goes up) and high P/Es to bear years (when the stock market goes down). In 2007, the average P/Es were low and expected to go even lower (which should spark a good run-up in share prices), but the subprime crisis poured water on the fire, and the markets ended the year essentially flat. On the other hand, even if you didn't know the first thing about average P/E, it didn't take a rocket scientist to sniff out the trouble with NASDAQ in 1999 and 2000 or the subprime mortgage crisis in 2006–2007.

In 2000, the People's Webby Award for best community was slash-dot.org (over CraigsList.com). Gomez.com won the Webby for best financial services site over the people's choice PayPal.com. Swoon.com competed with MarthaStewart.com for the Webby in the best living category. Sputnik7.com lost to Napster.com in music. Ever hear of half of these? And the one thing all of these sites had in common was that not one was making a penny. The NASDAQ run-up was all based on the fanciful notion that the companies of the New Economy didn't need to make money plus the hyped-up propaganda that if investors didn't buy in immediately, they'd never have another opportunity. Sound familiar?

Subprime borrowers (who, for the most part were real estate spec-ulators, not families) bought real estate at astronomically unafford-able prices with outlandish mortgage reset terms in 2005 and 2006. They originally bought in and hoped to flip for a profit before the bal-loon payment became due but ended up having to foreclose as early as 2007 when interest rates jumped and their teaser rates expired. Why did they buy in? Feverish demand was fueled by cheap, easy money. It was a very loose lending environment, and many investors believed (as they were told on television and in seminars) that they would get rich quick. Vulnerable investors overextended themselves because they were sold on the idea, by commission-based mortgage brokers, that the annual real estate gains would continue to soar, as they had between 2000 and 2005.

The reality was that real estate prices were out of affordability range in many markets in the United States beginning as early as 2005. In fact, without all of the fancy math tricks being done by aggressive mortgage lenders, far fewer buyers would have qualified to purchase at all. I know an illiterate fry cook who was being aggressively sold on a home loan he couldn't afford.

So, if it feels like you are paying a steep price for swampland just so that you don't miss the chance to own real estate and the gains that everyone is bragging about, chances are you are experiencing a bubble that is near to popping. Same thing if you're buying an Internet stock that no one has ever heard of that has been losing money for five years. No math skills needed. Just an extra large dose of common sense.

People who race to catch trends are chasing money. The same people who bought real estate on credit cards between 2005 and 2007 were buying stocks at the high in March of 2000—gamblers, not investors. You don't want to be dragging your nest egg on these wild goose chases! If you're trading on headlines, you're already too late!

Again, you won't have to worry so much about what the price of the general marketplace is this year when you are taking a 20- or 30-year view and are contributing monthly to your stock portfolio. Because you are contributing the same amount each month, you are constantly participating in new price points, rounding out the buy-in price and purchasing new holdings at the lower price (a very good thing). Tithing regularly and having a long-term strategy are the foundation of living the life of your dreams.

Of course, in your "buy low; sell high" Stocks-on-Steroids trading portfolio—that small percent of your nest egg where you take on higher risk for potentially higher gain—employing the average P/E of the general marketplace and the P/E of the company is critical.

AVERAGE PRICE-EARNINGS RATIO

P/E varies by industry, but as a general rule, the lower the number the better. Attractive average P/E values for the *general marketplace* are under 15. Average P/E values for the overall market are mid-range when they are at 18 and expensive at 20 or above.

The average P/E ratio of S&P Composite stocks was 20.3 in September 1987, before "Black Monday," when the Dow Jones Industrial

Average dropped 508 points, an alarming 22 percent. The average P/E was 30.50 in December of 1999, just months before the 2000–2002 recession kicked in. By comparison, the average P/E in the first quarter of 2007 was 17.

Now, I'm almost reluctant to give you these guideline numbers because price-to-earnings ratio is something that you're not going to really understand until you have had years of experience in the stock markets and have lived through a recession. Why? Because price-to-earnings ratio has two factors that affect the number. When earnings are poised to explode, then you can have a high price-to-earnings ratio that is actually a low price for the stock (because as the earnings side of the equation increases, the P/E ratio goes down). Thus, you have to be aware of current price *and* forward earnings potential in order to have an accurate picture of whether or not you're going to make money on your investment.

Gross Domestic Product (GDP) Growth

In late 2002, the average P/E in the S&P 500 was 32—very high; however, earnings were coming back and Gross Domestic Product growth was increasing. Thus, stock prices in the fourth quarter of 2002 were at the tipping point. What felt like the end of the world was actually the end of the bear market—the best buy-in point of a rally that kicked it up in 2003 and continued through late 2007. After October 2002, P/Es began to decline (a good thing), largely because of the increase in the earnings side of the equation. NASDAQ gained 45 percent in 2003.

In other words, GDP growth and earnings growth (or decline) will dramatically affect what happens to P/E, and those measurements are far more important to know when you are considering whether or not the stock prices are going to increase or decrease in value going forward. Stock prices have a high correlation with *following* earnings trends. When earnings increase, people get excited and buy, and the share price increases. When earnings go down, people freak out, sell and the price goes down. Thus, GDP growth measurements for the general marketplace, which dramatically effect earnings trends of the company, make a better crystal ball than the average P/E for the general marketplace.

How to Use Average P/E

If average P/Es get above 20 again, be cautious about what you buy, unless the economy is poised for a boom, as 20 average P/E means that investors are paying 20 or more times earnings on average for every stock—even those with little or no growth potential. You don't want to pay 20 times earnings for companies that only have an annual growth of 5 percent or less. It's overpriced and reckless. (Remember that there is still more to consider, which is why I say "be cautious" rather than don't do it.)

Now in July of 2007, the *average P/E* was 16. Companies still had excess cash reserves, with the industrials having over $600 billion, which was 6 percent of market value and a comfortable 40 percent of their long-term debt. Those who were worried about the weak U.S. dollar weren't considering that many of the publicly traded companies were by then operating in the global marketplace and were not overreliant on the U.S. dollar as the only currency. Earnings had been outstanding with double-digit operating growth for eighteen consecutive quarters, according to Standard and Poor's Senior Index Analyst, Howard Silverblatt. As a result, stocks performed very well through October of 2007, before the subprime mortgage crisis ground the economy to a standstill. (GDP growth for the fourth quarter of 2007 was 0.6 percent, down from 5 percent growth in the third quarter, according to the Bureau of Economic Analysis.)

Even before the BEA report was released in January of 2008, there were a lot of economists and policymakers who were using the R word—recession—predicting a dramatic slowing of growth, moderated earnings, less capital expenditures from business and lower consumer spending. When GDP growth stalls, stock prices decline. In that scenario, liquidity is very important (freeing up some cash by selling some stock before the down cycle), so that you can pick up holdings on your Stock Shopping List for lower prices later on in the recession cycle. In the buy low, sell high scenario, based on the forecast of continued decline in GDP growth, January 2008 might well be the high point of that year, just as March 2000 was the high of that election year.

To find out the current average GDP growth statistics, go to the U.S. Bureau of Economic Analysis at BEA.gov, which provides quarterly statistics on Gross Domestic Product and Gross National Product growth.

EARNINGS GROWTH IN INDIVIDUAL COMPANIES

When the general marketplace is poised to do well, you don't have to be as nervous about buying individual *growth* companies, like Google, at a high P/E. Google's *top line revenue* rocketed up in the second quarter of 2007 a robust 58 percent. The earnings side of the P/E was moving even faster than investors were buying in. If you bought at the 52-week low of $400, when the P/E was about 50, you would have done great later on in the year when Google traded for above $740 per share.

As another case in point, you would have done great in 1987—the year of Black Monday—if you bought another growth stock, Microsoft, at a 20 P/E. (Microsoft's IPO was in 1986.) You would not have done so well with buying Ford (a large blue-chip stock) at that time. As an old legacy company with limited annual growth, Ford would have to have a considerably lower P/E or be trading for a song—to make it a worthy selection.

So, how can you tell when a company is experiencing rapid growth in the earnings side of the P/E equation? The simplest way is to check the "Financials" page of the stock on your favorite financial web site. Many line up the revenue by quarter and year, so it's very easy to see which number is bigger (or smaller) and by how much. Sales that are rapidly increasing are a very good sign. Declining sales are a red flag. In the earnings reports, the companies, typically, even do the math for you, letting you know the percentage of gains (or losses) by quarter and by year, often with an explanation from the CEO as to why. Be sure to check both sales and income (how much the company is making after expenses), since the company is going to emphasize the one that looks the best in the earnings press release.

Google's revenue growth went from just under a billion in 2003 to $6 billion by year-end 2005 and racked up more than $15 billion in sales in 2007. Opsware's revenue growth went from $61 million in 2006 to $101.7 million in fiscal year 2007 and is on track to continue growing apace with Cisco and Hewlett-Packard distributing their software. (Hewlett-Packard owns the company now.) Both companies had incredible growth, and I found that information by using two clicks on my favorite financial web site.

THE HARE WINS THE DASH; JABBA THE HUTT
RULES THE UNIVERSE

Is there another way to separate the slow, steady companies from the fast-growing companies? In short, the bigger the company, typically the slower the revenue growth due to increased competition and market saturation. The smaller and younger the company, the faster the growth, especially if it's in a new, hot industry and has the best product in that space. There is greater potential for gains in small cap companies, which can justify paying a higher P/E and sometimes even buying in before the company is profitable (with a P/E of N/A).

I refer to hot, young companies as "the hare" and steady, reliable companies—like General Electric, Microsoft and other big, fat blue chips—as Jabba the Hutt. The hare can win the dash and make you very happy and rich in the short run; Jabba the Hutt wins the marathon and adds stability to the foundation of your nest egg. Keeping the small growth company well fed and fiscally fit requires a lot of tending. If you're not willing to do the research and keep your eye on the temperature of the sector, the cash on hand, the earnings growth, the insider trading and/or the deal flow, you might miss cashing in your gains.

Jabba the Hutt rules the universe and wins the marathon. If he gains or loses a pound or two in the meantime, you're not going to notice much. There is much less gain or loss or spectacular movements in share price in these big companies, which can be a very stabilizing force for your nest egg but a frustrating presence in a trading portfolio. And if the hare is winning every race in their field, Jabba the Hutt companies will either gobble up the hare (acquire the company), step on the hare (beat them with a price war or other competitive tactic), sideline the hare (tie up the executives with legal wrangling) or utilize some other trick to win back the profits.

In short, for your trading portfolio, where you are looking to take your profits in shorter windows, the smaller, younger, fast-growth companies are really going to afford the highest returns (with higher volatility and more risk as well). You'll want some Jabba the Hutts in your long-term portfolio for the stability (as well as some hares for growth). The easiest way to identify the two in your retirement plan is that hares are called "small caps," and Jabbas are called "big caps." If you have small, medium and big caps with both value and growth stocks, then you are diversifying—a good thing for long-term investing.

SELLING HIGH

The part of the equation that many people miss most frequently is the *sell high* part. One person I know was advised by his accountant not to sell Sun Microsystems at $95 in 2000 because he was in a high tax bracket, had made a very large gain in the stock and would have to pay high taxes on the capital gains. The accountant advised that it was a much better idea to transfer the stock into a trust for his three children, and he took that advice. This man would have netted $600,000 *after* taxes from selling. Over the next two years, Sun fell to $5.00 per share. Seven years later, the price of Sun shares were still trading at $5, having lost over 90 percent of its value.

It's hard to justify not selling when the owner of the stock could have cashed out, paid the taxes *and* given the three children $200,000 each. Instead, the three children have spent seven years holding onto stock with a combined value of only $22,000—all because their dad listened to advice that was based on trying to avoid paying taxes on the capital gains.

NEGATIVE EARNINGS IN YOUNG COMPANIES VERSUS DISTRESSED COMPANIES

It's not uncommon to see the P/E listed as "N/A," which means the company is losing money. That isn't necessarily a bad thing. MySpace.com had negative earnings when it was gobbled up by News Corp., rewarding many investors a fantastic return on their money. I featured MySpace.com's parent company in my April 2005 e-zine when it was trading at $7.49 per share, and Rupert Murdoch purchased the social networking giant for $12.00 per share the following September, providing a 60 percent gain in under six months.

When Opsware announced that they were being acquired by Hewlett-Packard on July 23, 2007, for $14.25 per share, the company was still producing negative earnings—in other words, had a P/E of N/A—after five years of operations. My newsletter had featured Opsware in 2002 when it was trading for just $1.80, so investors who purchased after our article was published saw a return of 690 percent in just five years.

So, negative earnings (or N/A P/E) in young companies can be just fine, whereas negative earnings in a large legacy corporation, like Delta Airlines and United Airlines had before their bankruptcies and Ford Motor Company and General Motors had in January 2008, typically spells trouble. After decades of doing business, if a corporation starts losing money, that means that something has gone very wrong—either consumers are no longer buying the product, costs are staggering or both. GM and Ford investors took big losses between 2004 and 2007. Common shareholders of Delta and United stock lost everything when the companies restructured under Chapter 11.

Many very troubled companies—particularly in the airline business, but also in auto parts like Delphi and other aging industries—are using Chapter 11 to restructure their expenses, particularly their pension plan and other post-employment benefits (OPEBs), like health care, so it is a risky proposition to be an investor in a legacy company that is losing money, especially those seeking union concessions. Investing in distressed companies that are losing money is best left to the institutional professionals who, because of their large purchases, are able to negotiate preferential treatment of their stock in the event of a Chapter 11 scenario. Common stock investors end up with wallpaper when a company goes into bankruptcy. The corporation, when/if it emerges from bankruptcy, issues new stock to new investors, offering no compensation to the common shareholders of the old stock, whereas bondholders and institutional investors typically strike a better deal.

GROWTH VERSUS VALUE

If you consider future earnings *growth* potential, then, as I've indicated throughout this chapter and elsewhere, a higher (or even negative) P/E can still be a good value if the earnings are increasing rapidly. Thus, both *value* (buying at the lowest price possible) and *growth* (increasing earnings) matter.

This is why small cap value funds, investing in smaller companies with lots of hyper-charged growth potential that are trading for a song, tend to be the best performers on Wall Street (and certainly something you should have in your long-term portfolio).

IT'S COUNTERINTUITIVE!

"Buy low, sell high" sounds so easy, but the most important thing to remember is that it's counterintuitive. With "buy low, sell high," *what you feel* is almost always going to lead you astray (until you retrain your emotions to serve you rather than rule you). You're going to *want* to sell after 9/11 and during the worst days of the subprime crisis. You're going to *feel pressure* to buy Internet stocks the year *after* rock-star gains, like in 2000. You're going to be tempted to jump blindly into a risky loan when real estate has doubled overnight.

Yes, "buy low, sell high" is running against the herd, and yet, it's not as easy as declaring that you'll be a "contrarian" investor. Contrarian means that you're counting headlines instead of reading GDP growth reports, where the meat and potatoes of the economy are served. You'll get more information by sticking to your Stock Report Cards and Four Questions than you will by obsessively reading the news or trying to get your Ph.D. in statistics. The nonstop news is either bad news or gossip, whereas the good guys, who are flying under the radar, are the ones producing the greatest gains. When it comes to your money and where you invest it, stick with those things you know and care about, rather than think you can outwit the marketplace by doing the opposite of what everyone is doing.

APPLYING AVERAGE P/E TO YOUR NEST-EGG PORTFOLIO

The strategies you use for buy/sell decisions in your riskier Stocks-on-Steroids portfolio don't work so well for the long-term portion of your investments. Here's how the strategies differ.

Buying/Selling in your Nest Egg

With regard to your long-term holdings, it's a good idea to evaluate your investments at least twice a year and monitor any big news on the general marketplace steadily, but not obsessively. (Obsessive news watching can make you paranoid, which is a very bad foundation for successful investing.)

As Sallie Krawcheck, the chairman and CEO of Citigroup's Global Wealth Management, says, "What your financial services provider should be doing is not to get you in and out of segments of the market on a rapid-fire basis, but to give you a diversified portfolio. When the stock market goes up, you take some profits out. When fixed income goes up, tilt it that way." By having predetermined biannual checkups with your financial services partner, you take the fever out of investing and ensure that you are pruning the limbs of your money tree for a better harvest.

Cash Is King

Probably the most common way of losing money in your nest egg is to be forced to sell at a loss when your stocks should just be sitting in your portfolio waiting for the markets to turn. The reason this occurs is that during a recession, people lose jobs, credit becomes more difficult to obtain and expensive to pay back and the stress of the financial crisis might cause health problems. The way to avoid having to sell low during a recession—the one thing that gets you through any down cycle, whether it's in real estate, stocks and bonds or just a personal tragedy—is having your assets properly allocated. You should always keep a percent equal to your age safe and liquid, that is, not invested in the stock market.

Having enough cash on hand to pay your bills means never having to liquidate your holdings at a loss. You don't want to be forced to sell low just to keep the bill collectors away. Getting through hard times is probably the real key to successful investing! And with the four D's of life—death, depression, divorce and disaster—you want to provide for the unexpected in case you are forced to reduce your hours or even stop working.

The other added benefit of valuing "cash is king" is that you are poised to be a buyer with plenty of cash on hand in the event of a major drop in the share price of companies you love or at the point that the market is turning from a recession back into growth. The hardest part about buying low is having the funds in a harsh environment—such as a recession—and recognizing value where others don't see it. Most people don't think ahead and are left kicking themselves when great things go on sale that they don't have the ability to buy.

THE BOTTOM LINE

Good luck trying to explain price-earnings ratio to your friends when lower is better most of the time, higher can be great in some cases, even negative earnings are okay in the right scenario and high average price-to-earnings ratios in 2000 were more worrisome than an even higher average P/E in January 2003. Your best strategy in a game that has produced annualized gains of over 10 percent every year, but has such unpredictability in the short-term? Turn off the television. Stop trying to out-think the Nobel Laureates. Take a long view. Relax and enjoy your money! And when/if you do pick individual companies, make sure that you have a hundred reasons why, that you have lined the company up with the competition in a Stock Report Card and that you are buying low and selling high.

NATALIE'S THREE TAKEAWAY TIPS

1. GDP growth is more closely tied with market performance than average price-to-earnings ratios.
2. You won't have to worry so much about what the price of the general marketplace is this year when you are taking a 20- or 30-year view and are contributing monthly to your stock portfolio. Because you are contributing the same amount each month, you are constantly participating in new price points, rounding out the buy-in price.
3. Companies that experience rapid growth, as Google and Opsware did between 2002 and 2007, can have a higher price-to-earnings ratio or even a negative price-to-earnings ratio when they first start out, because the earnings side of the equation is growing rapidly and will eventually bring down the P/E ratio.

OPTIONS: MAKE SURE YOU CAN HIT THE BALL OVER THE NET BEFORE ATTEMPTING

Physics has three laws that explain 99 percent of the phenomena, and economics has 99 laws that explain 3 percent of the phenomena.

—PROFESSOR ANDREW LO,
MIT SLOAN SCHOOL OF MANAGEMENT

"Trading options isn't easy," according to eTrade's tutorial on options, yet there are dozens of sites, if not hundreds, fervently trying to convince you that options trading is not only easy but also a cheap way to "make more money."

One company claims that there's "No need to waste time crunching numbers. With a few quick clicks [our company] does it all for you, presented in tables for easy comparison." Another claims to have "Options Trading software that predicts with 80 percent acccurcy." (We guess it also spells with 80 percent accuracy.)

So, the companies selling you software for hundreds and thousands of dollars tell you it is easy, but that is simply *untrue*. In fact, according to economist Kevin Murphy, the George J. Stigler Distinguished Professor of Economics at the University of Chicago Graduate School of Business and a Senior Fellow at the Milken Institute, 97 percent of hedge fund managers, who are the best and brightest on Wall Street, can't even outperform the market by 3 percent on a consistent basis.

How likely is it that a company that can't even spell right on its web site is going to do better?

Commodity, futures and options traders have been responsible for the most colossal losses on Wall Street. The Bank of Montreal announced on May 17, 2007, that experienced commodity traders at their bank had lost $680 million when the volatility on natural gas trading flattened out. In 2007, Bear Stearns fired a copresident (who had been with the firm for most of his career) for subprime mortgage investment losses. According to *The Wall Street Journal*, two of Bear Stearns mortgage-related hedge funds blew up, costing investors more than $1 billion. In March of 2008, J. P. Morgan bailed out Bear Stearns for $2/share.

The Bank of Montreal fired the traders responsible for taking on that kind of risk; then they restructured their trading desk and suspended their relationship with Optionable, Inc., the options broker that had handled the trades. Optionable responded by saying basically that it wasn't their fault. Albert Helmig, the company chairman, said, "We are never pleased when losses dominate for one of our clients, but we do not design or help to design their strategies, nor are we financial advisors."

If you lose, don't expect the company that sold you the software to bail you out with a check, and trying to win back losses in court usually costs more than it's worth. Even if you are awarded pennies on the dollar of your losses, that might be dwarfed by the mountain of costs in time, money, prescription medications and doctor bills. Lawsuits are expensive, ugly, stressful and often an enormous negative drain on your wallet, spirit and health. No matter how much the company has advertised the ease of its trading platform, charts and research data, there are also ample disclaimers that your losses are your fault.

There has been a tremendous amount of volatility in the markets over the past six years (a good thing for experienced options traders). The period has seen trends reverse themselves multiple times, much to the shock and chagrin of professionals and novices alike (not so good for software-based strategies).

So are you a complete dummy to invest in options? Not according to Dr. Myron Scholes, a Nobel-winning economist and the chairman of Oak Hill Platinum Partners. Dr. Scholes suggests that if you're smart with options, you can have the best of both worlds—a safe portfolio, with the power to strike rich returns. He advised the crowd at the 2006 Milken Conference that "Options are wonderful things. . . . You can put 10 percent of your money in call options, and 90 percent in bonds. You've got the upside—options—with 90 percent of the money safe."

It should be noted that Dr. Scholes cocreated the Black-Scholes options pricing model and that Oak Hill Platinum Partners is a hedge fund. His bias toward options is quite natural; he is an expert and understands all of the risks and rewards as well as how to evaluate the best opportunities out there. Dr. Scholes literally wrote the book on options. But all of that wisdom and experience and all those accolades didn't save Long-Term Capital—Dr. Scholes's hedge fund that collapsed in 1998—from going bankrupt.

HEDGE FUNDS

Hedge funds are loosely regulated, privately held investment vehicles designed for aggressive investing by very wealthy individuals. You have to be a qualified, experienced investor/millionaire and agree to a lock-out period during which you cannot withdraw your money in order to participate in one. My advice on this is simple: 99 percent of the people reading this book should not be putting money into a hedge fund. If you do go with a hedge fund, the manager needs 10 times the due diligence and background check as you would give a broker, and the returns the manager boasts of should be verified and consistent over a minimum period of seven years.

I'm not singling Dr. Scholes out to pick on him. I'm highlighting his quote as an illustration that even smart people can say silly things. Imagine an aggressive commodity salesperson using that quote to commandeer your interest in buying his securities!

Few financial professionals would recommend having 90 percent in bonds and 10 percent in options, and *never* for a new investor. In fact, most brokerages will not even allow you to trade options at all until you've been trading for at least a year. With options, you lose most or all of your investment if you're not "in the money" when the option expires, which can be as soon as a few days or as long as a few years, depending on the expiration date you select.

So if limit orders, puts, calls and strike price are still hieroglyphics to you, start with the ABCs of investing before you try to outtalk and outmaneuver the Nobel Laureates on Wall Street. The Chicago Board Options Exchange offers the most reputable tutorial for options trading. Go to CBOE.com for more information. Education and practicing in fictitious scenarios first are the best ways to increase your odds of measurable gains.

Remember that trading options is a tennis match. You wouldn't wager on beating Roger Federer at tennis until you became good enough to serve a few aces that blew right past him. If you think you're the next Ivan Ljubicic, who hit 273 more aces than Federer in 2006, then that's the time you step on the court and get your game on.

The primary problem of options is the expiration date. One of the most important factors for "selling high" is determining your best time to sell. Options trading limits your selling opportunity to a narrow window, which means that you have to be right *and* the market has to agree with you within a very narrow time frame to come out ahead. Buying stock, on the other hand, allows one the freedom to hold on and ride out any volatile waves that might occur in the stock price of the company you believe in.

THE BOTTOM LINE

You'll get all kinds of sales pitches on options as "insurance" or as an easy way to make a lot more money. When options programs are hawked on newbie investors, the only person making money is the software manufacturer and the salesperson. Be just as wary of salesmen touting the millions you'll make overnight on oil and gas or futures on corn and pork bellies.

NATALIE'S THREE TAKEAWAY TIPS

1. Options trading is not easy and is absolutely **not** for beginners. Even experienced hedge fund managers have had huge losses trading options.
2. Options trading software companies say that their software predicts with 80 percent accuracy. That claim has nothing to do with how much money their clients make. For true measurements on how **successful** a strategy is, you need to see the actual annualized gains earned **over time** by every single client (something the company will never provide you with). Many money managers and companies will quote cumulative gains, which must be divided by the number of years in order to get an idea of what the gains each year are. For instance, 50 percent cumulative gains for ten years is less than 5 percent gain per year. That is not very impressive when the stock market performance is, on average, over double that return, with far less risk and work.
3. Options trading limits the amount of time that you have to make a return on investment. When the option expires, you can lose all of your investment if you are not "in the money."

LESSONS FROM ENRON

57.73% of employees' 401(k) assets were invested in Enron stock as it fell 98.8% in value during 2001. But employees at many companies still have even larger percentages of their 401(k) assets in company stock than Enron employees did.
—FINRA.org INVESTOR ALERT

Power. There's no doubt that Enron had power. Kenneth Lay, the founder, chairman and CEO of Enron, was one of the most connected businessmen in the United States, with personal ties to President George W. Bush and Vice President Dick Cheney. His power on Capitol Hill was real, but his $100 billion power business turned out to be a bust.

What's more important to the average investor is that, as Enron chief whistle-blower and former vice president Sherron Watkins says, "It can happen again." Investors can swoon over a company's grand achievements, invest manically in what they think is a once-in-a-lifetime opportunity and end up bitter and broke from the whole sordid affair. And the most sobering aspect of it all is that Enron was the most highly respected company in America prior to its demise, winning *Fortune* magazine's Most Innovative Company award six years in a row and consistently topping analysts' recommendation lists.

Before you abandon Wall Street altogether, remember that Enron was one rotten apple among thousands of fruitful, honest companies, and there were plenty of warning signs that Enron was a fraud. The majority of publicly traded companies run clean operations. There are over 5,000 corporations traded on Wall Street, and in 2003, only

354 restated their earnings. Of those, only a handful turned out to be in a class with Enron or Worldcom.

Most of the problems with Enron were easy to discover for anyone who cared enough to inquire beyond the headlines and analyst recommendations. As Richard Furlin, president of Furlin Financial and a former senior director at Standard & Poor's says, "There weren't just red flags, but banners and skyrockets. The problem was that the so-called watch dogs—auditors, stock analysts and so on—had little motivation to expose the problems."

Here's a timeline of some of the highlights, red flags and skyrockets declaring trouble:

ENRON TIMELINE

1999
- *Fortune* names Enron as one of the 25 best places to work in America.

2000
- 96 percent of Enron's revenue comes not from the natural gas and pipelines business that the company was founded on, but from trading.
- 80 percent of revenues ($100 billion) come from businesses that were new in the last five years. (What five-year-old business do you know that generates $80 billion in revenue? Not even Google and Microsoft combined were doing that in 2008.)
- Enron's annual report shows $101 billion in revenue, $10.5 billion in debt.
- The company was included on *Fortune* magazine's Platinum 400 List for revenue in excess of $100 billion.

- Kenneth Lay receives $135 million from salary, bonus and stock options.[1]
- December 28. At $84.87/share, Enron becomes the seventh most valuable U.S. company.

2001

- February 6. Enron wins *Fortune*'s "Most Innovative Company" award for the sixth year in a row.
- March 5. *Fortune* reporter Bethany McLean writes, "The company remains largely impenetrable to outsiders. How exactly does Enron make its money? Details are hard to come by. . . . Analysts don't seem to have a clue." (*Huge* red flag that everyone ignored.)
- April 17. Enron reports a 281 percent increase in quarterly revenues to $50 billion and a 20 percent increase in net income to $406 million over the previous year. (Having one of the world's largest corporations report so vast an increase in quarterly revenues occurs about as often as hell freezing over. Large corporations simply have too much competition to increase revenues to that extreme, and new lines of business just don't have the volume to increase sales that rapidly.)
- May. Vice Chairman Clifford Baxter leaves the firm after clashing with Skilling over accounting practices.[2]
- August 14. CEO Jeffrey Skilling resigns, citing "personal reasons," exercising options for $66 million.[3] (*Big* red flag.) Kenneth Lay becomes CEO again.
- August 15. Sherron Watkins sends a letter to Kenneth Lay warning of accounting irregularities.

---

1. *Forbes.*
2. The reason for his departure is from Sherron Watkins.
3. As cited in the motion picture *Enron: The Smartest Guys in the Room.*

- August 20. Kenneth Lay cashes in Enron share options worth $519,000.
- August 21. Kenneth Lay cashes in Enron share options worth $1.48 million. (Skyrocket)
- October 11. Accounting firm Andersen and Andersen shreds Enron audit documents.
- October 16. Enron reports losses of $638 million from operations between July and September and announces a $1.2 billion reduction in shareholder equity. (Skyrocket)
- November 8. Enron revises five years of financial statements. Instead of massive profits, the company reports losing $586 million. (Skyrocket)
- November 9. Dynegy announces takeover of Enron for $8 billion in shares.
- November 19. Enron warns that it needs $690 million for debt due by the end of the month.
- November 21. Enron trades at $5.33/share, down from $85 less than a year earlier.
- November 28. Enron bonds are downgraded to junk bond status.
- November 29. Enron trades at $1.52/share.
- December 2. Enron files for bankruptcy.

2002
- January 10. Attorney General John Ashcroft and a 100-strong team of federal investigators arrive in Houston for an Enron probe.
- January 16. Enron is delisted.
- January 23. Kenneth Lay resigns.
- January 25. Clifford Baxter, former vice chairman and chief strategy officer, commits suicide.

2003–2006

- Kenneth Lay and Jeffrey Skilling are free on bail, awaiting their trials.

2006

- May 26. A federal jury finds Jeffrey Skilling and Kenneth Lay guilty of fraud and conspiracy.
- July 5. Kenneth Lay is found dead.

Let's start with the first red flag that Enron was a train wreck waiting to happen—the stench of greed so revolting it reeked all the way from Texas to California despite the awards it was winning in business magazines.

Amid paeans of praise for Enron's made-up earnings and its prestigious awards prior to the blowup, there was one lone naysayer whose voice was publicly heard—Bethany McLean of *Fortune* magazine, reporting in March 2001. Merrill Lynch analyst John Olsen was fired when he announced that he would downgrade Enron. The consulting group Off Wall Street recommended a short sell on Enron in May of 2001, but the information was marketed for a premium to money managers only and was not publicly available.

Meanwhile, California was experiencing power outages. Prices of utilities were so high that senior citizens who couldn't afford to air-condition their homes were dying. Wildfires were raging in the hills of Southern California. Traders at Enron, and the *publicly available* Enron literature—brochures and earnings reports—boasted of how their company was able to capitalize on peak energy prices that could be sold thousands of times higher than normal without once acknowledging that vulnerable people might die as a result of that blind avarice. Price gouging of this nature was the reason that energy prices were regulated to begin with. California Governor Gray Davis was livid with Enron's policies and sued the company.

Whether the other analysts and journalists were fooled by the bravado and the impressive facade created by the chief executives at Enron or just playing along to appease their bosses, your own nose could have sniffed out that something was rotten in Texas (where Enron was based). If the investment you're considering is winning hearts and minds of consumers (Enron certainly wasn't) and producing products or services that real people *love* firsthand, chances are that the company and the management team are not going to be producing *Enron: the Sequel*. The employees at the company are telling you what you need to know most about the company—that it's good enough for them to produce the best products on the planet in their industry. "Beloved" is not a word that Enron's customers would use to describe their feelings toward the company; a good deal of the "products" that Enron boasted of having earnings on were a pipe dream.

That is how you can see through the impressive awards, overnights in the Lincoln Bedroom at the White House, outstanding headlines and a workplace that even Enron whistleblower Sherron Watkins called "exciting." Greed has been a constant theme throughout humanity. You can regulate it, prosecute it, punish it and somehow it still finds a way in the few soul-dead individuals who believe money and power equal happiness. You can't kill greed, but you can educate yourself to spot warning signs and successfully identify the Gordon Gekkos from the Ghandis. There were plenty of red flags that were flying at Enron months before the company imploded.

TWELVE RED FLAG LESSONS FROM ENRON

If you see the Twelve Red Flags and Skyrocket signs listed below in a company in which you're interested in investing, you'd be wise to move on, no matter how hot the stock is on Wall Street or how many awards the corporation and its executives have won.

Red Flag #1: A company executive asks for blind faith.

When you think about it, not even church leaders ask you to go strictly on blind faith. When asked for evidence of a God, they can respond, "Angelina Jolie." When asked for evidence of earnings, Jeffrey Skilling called the inquisitive analyst "an a**hole" and later said, "It's difficult to show how money goes in and out of Enron—particularly in wholesale." If a company can't explain something as fundamental as earnings in language you can understand, be suspicious.

Red Flag #2: The company makes unreasonable growth claims.

"Explosive Earnings in the World's 7th Largest Corporation." Going from $40 billion in revenue in 1999 to $100 billion the following year is the equivalent of claiming that Jabba the Hutt can run the 100-yard dash in less than four seconds. Moving that fast with that kind of girth is against at least four hundred laws of human nature and business, and you're right to think that story is a great basis for a comedy, provided you aren't the one crushed under the weight of the fall. By the time a company is fat enough to attract $40 billion in revenue, the market is well established, competitors have found a way to yank some of the customers to their corner and the staff of inexperienced newbies has grown substantially.

Red Flag #3: Consensus Insider Selling: Company insiders are unloading stock.

Liars will say anything, but their actions reveal everything. Check the insider trader activity on your favorite financial web site to see what the insiders really believe about their company. Four key Enron executives had resigned and cashed out millions between 2000 and 2001 *before* Jeffrey Skilling jumped ship. Kenneth Lay sold $2 million in stock the week *after* Sherron Watkins warned him of "accounting irregularities." This was a month before Lay tried to reassure investors and employees that Enron stock was an "incredible bargain." Most financial web sites update the insider trading activity daily. The SEC.gov web site lists all reported insider trading activity.

Red Flag #4: The rats are jumping overboard.

The executive exodus at Enron began in 2000, and by the time Jeffrey Skilling resigned in August of the following year, almost all of Kenneth Lay's key team had taken the money and run. Kenneth Rice, chairman of Enron Broadband, resigned in August 2001. Lou Pai, chairman of Enron Energy Services, cashed out $270 million[4] and left in 2000. Joe Sutton cashed out $42 million and left in November of 2000. Clifford Baxter, vice chairman, resigned in May 2001, three months before Jeffrey Skilling. According to Skilling, Mr. Baxter was resigning to spend more time with his family. But Sherron Watkins wrote in her August 2001 letter to Kenneth Lay that Mr. Baxter complained "mightily" to Skilling and "all who would listen" about the shady accounting tactics that the company was using to hide debt and inflate earnings. Additionally, Jeffrey Skilling had been grooming himself for the CEO position at Enron for years, but after just six months of his dream-come-true job, he announced that he was throwing in the towel for "personal reasons." Right. Just as you know that "irreconcilable differences" hides the truth of why a marriage failed, you know that "personal reasons" hides a slew of juicy details as to why a corporate relationship blew up.

Red Flag #5: Jack of all trades; master of none.

Kenneth Lay, Jeffrey Skilling and Vice Chairman Joe Sutton opened their joint letter to shareholders in 1999 with the following: "Enron is moving so fast that sometimes others have trouble defining us." Red flag. Moving fast for the space shuttle is pretty exciting. Moving fast in a thousand different directions is hardly the best business model. Success-

---

4. Lou Pai's stock sale is as reported by *Forbes*.

ful companies find something that they do well and perfect it—from product to profit margins—before expanding into *related* industries.

The Enron executives boasted that "Enron often introduces a product before the competition even senses a market exists. Cross-commodity trading, weather derivatives, energy outsourcing and 1999's two major initiatives—EnronOnline and Enron Broadband Services—demonstrate our resourcefulness." The letter is littered with the term "First-Mover Advantage" and is largely bereft of the details on growth, infrastructure, sales, Return On Investment and other basic elements of a successful new business proposition. In the 1999 report, Enron claimed first-mover advantage in online innovation (predicting that they would outperform Intel in their first year of business), in weather, energy trading, oil in Spain, coal in Poland, weather derivatives in France, natural gas in the U.K., power plants in Poland, Turkey, Sardinia, Croatia and Spain, wind power in California, Germany and Spain, pulp and paper and even emissions derivatives. But how can a staff of pipe and gas people outperform the experts of those diverse fields in all of those different countries? Any detail-oriented, inquisitive investor would have known enough to pass.

Red Flag #6: Unrealistic expansion claims.
According to Enron, their power plant in India, which was still under construction at the time of Enron's bankruptcy, would serve as a "cornerstone for a vast India energy network that will serve as a springboard for multiple Enron businesses, including broadband services, in the region." In 2002, the year that Enron declared bankruptcy, less than five in one hundred Indians used the Internet—some 5 million Internet users scattered across a land area of a million square miles, with 71.9 percent of the population living in the sticks.[5] Broadband was still less popular than dial-up in the United States! The economics

---

5. Milken Institute.

of trying to connect large numbers of Indians who don't even own a computer simply didn't compute.

How about electricity? A quarter of the Indian population lives in desperate poverty and can't afford to pay for energy. And enterprising Indians, even those with little education, have learned how to tap the power lines to access electricity without paying (as some Americans do with their neighbor's Wi-Fi).

Common sense and a layman's knowledge of the Indian nation should have been telling market analysts and astute investors that there couldn't be the markets in India to support Enron's asinine claims.

Red Flag #7: The company is loathed by its customers.

California Governor Gray Davis got a standing ovation during his inaugural address for his war with Enron; however, he wasn't able to win the battle fast enough to save his job. After Davis was voted out of office in the middle of his second term, the truth came out that the power blackouts had been due to Enron manipulating the supply of electricity to boost their revenues. According to local news reports, people in California had actually died from the heat when their airconditioning stopped working. Others were trapped in elevators for hours during rolling brownouts. Wrongful death is about as low as it goes in customer loathing. If Enron hadn't imploded, it's very likely the company would be buried in class action lawsuits.

Red Flag #8: The company is no longer making its money from its core business.

In 2000, Enron was earning over 90 percent of its (inflated) earnings not from its core business of pipelines and natural gas but from hedging. If the core business model isn't providing revenue and the company is using financial tricks to stay alive, it's time to abandon ship. Companies like Enron that gamble with shareholder dollars and employee retirement funds are exposing everyone to fiscal fallout.

Red Flag #9: Bulls make money, bears make money, pigs get slaughtered.

Enron's P/E of 33 was double that of Goldman Sachs's and *way* too high for an energy company (the industry standard P/E for utilities is under 10). Even if the investor had missed the prior eight red flags, s/he might have known to take her profits just by noticing the high P/E. And here is where investing in a company that you care about will give you the competitive edge. You'll be thinking about the company, checking up on it, reading about it, learning everything you can about it and so be much more likely to notice when the P/E gets way too high. It can be that simple. Have an investment strategy that includes profit taking when a corporation's share price looks more expensive than it's worth.

Red Flag #10: "Greed is good."

Enron's own shareholder literature boasts that during the California energy crisis, the company was able to "successfully capture the high margins of Summer 1999." The California Blackouts and Brownouts of 1999 dramatically impacted the lives of Californians. Seniors went without food trying to afford electric bills that had increased one-hundred-fold overnight. Commuters were injured or killed in traffic accidents because the streetlights were out. Brush fires destroyed homes. Further, according to some of California's energy officials, none of the alleged shortages made any sense, and taped documentation that was included in the movie *Enron: The Smartest Guys in the Room* suggests that some Enron traders masterminded blackouts to bring in income for the company (and commissions for themselves).

Make sure that you can take having the blood of grandmothers on your hands before you invest in a company with that kind of ethos. You'll find the corporate philosophy in the annual earnings report that is issued to shareholders. This report usually opens with a letter from the CEO. The CEO is the soul of the company, so her plain language can be a very reliable indicator of the underlying vision of how the company is run.

Red Flag #11: Company inflates own stock.

Enron encouraged its employees to invest in company stock, matching half of their 401(k) contributions in Enron stock as an incentive. According to FINRA.org, 57 percent of employees' 401(k) assets were invested in Enron stock as it lost 99 percent of its value. As a result, many Enron employees lost their income, job *and* retirement plan in one fell swoop.

Never have a large percent of your investments in any one thing and certainly not in the company you work for. Also, if you get wind of a company that does that, know that they are inflating the market value of their own company in an unprofessional and potentially illegal way. FINRA guidelines are that employees should not have more than 10 to 20 percent of their nest egg in stock in the company they work for.

Red Flag #12: Analyst recommendations defy common sense.

As in all walks of life, there are good analysts and bad analysts. There are analysts with a moral spine and others who are just trying to pay for their kids' private school and braces. There are analysts who can be pressured to give favorable recommendations, and those like John Olsen, the analyst of Merrill Lynch who was fired for not recommending Enron, who place integrity first. As a general rule, I read the analyst reports of my favorite market professionals *only* for the charts and data, and I completely ignore their recommendations. Brokerages have investment banking relationships with the corporations that they analyze. With *so* many competing interests working behind the scenes, you can never be quite sure whether a recommendation to buy is someone's ticket into a Manhattan private school. If all of the red flags are present but the analyst's report in front of you is saying the opposite, trust your analysis over hers. Bethany McLean did.

THE BOTTOM LINE

Power. It's intoxicating. Now you know how to avoid getting drunk.

By the way: *Enron: The Smartest Guys in the Room* is a must-see film for any investor. Rent it.

NATALIE'S THREE TAKEAWAY TIPS

1. The CEO is the soul of the company.
2. Executive exodus at a corporation is a huge red flag that something is amiss. A smooth succession plan—such as occurred at Disney when COO Bob Iger replaced former CEO Michael Eisner—is different than executives jumping ship with their golden parachutes and a bag of loot claiming that they "want to spend more time with their families."
3. The products and services of the corporation tell you a lot more about how well the company is doing than the awards that the company might be receiving.

TOP ELEVEN SIGNS THE CEO IS ROLLING IN YOUR DOUGH

The CEO is the soul of the company.
—KAY KOPLOVITZ, FOUNDER, USA NETWORKS

The majority of CEOs on Wall Street are hardworking, honest men and women. The Enron, Worldcom and Tyco debacles are not the norm. Bad news = *beaucoup* television advertising sales, so news programs love splashing the sordid details of scandal on their headlines. But that doesn't mean that something seedy is happening in every corporate suite across America. At the same time, the executives who do end up behind bars have a surprising number of characteristics in common. They tend to be the most aggressive about bending the rules.

CEO/cheerleaders can seduce investors (and win positive headlines) with legal loopholes and sleight-of-hand tricks even if they never technically cross the line of lying, cheating or stealing. The company may have red bleeding all over its balance sheets, inching toward bankruptcy, but by airbrushing the troubled areas and applying some makeup to the product line, journalists and even respected analysts can be bamboozled into reporting on the "good news" that diverts attention away from the true story.

This is another situation where cowboys (with a nose for BS) can have a leg up on the city slicker (who relies on newspapers for information). No journalist was reporting that you couldn't get a simple garden tool at Kmart when my father experienced that firsthand. No headlines warned about the telecommunications industry imploding on rock-bottom long distance rates when I, as a neophyte investor, added up that revenue sinkholes cannot be earnings geysers.

THE TOP ELEVEN SIGNS A CEO IS ROLLING IN YOUR DOUGH, COOKING THE BOOKS, DILLYDALLYING, HOBKNOBBING OR PLAYING TIDDLYWINKS

In this section I'll show you the top warning signs that a company or CEO is being a little too freewheeling or too loose with the company checkbook or, worse, that the whole company ship is sinking. If you see one or more of these signs in a company, take note and put the information in the "Cons of Investing" side of the equation. If you see a slew of signs, it's probably best to move on to another choice.

1. Rock Star CEO

When the CEO shows up more often in the society pages than in the executive suite, the company's bottom line is taking a mud bath on your dime. Now, there's nothing wrong with Nike building a brand around Andre Agassi or Michael Jordan or the RED ad campaign having Penelope Cruz as a cover girl. But when you start noticing an executive repeatedly in the background of party photos, that's a different story. Long before Sam Waksal, the former chairman and CEO of IMClone, was convicted of insider trading, he was a frequent face in the Hamptons society pages, often pictured next to one very famous rock star.

Too much tippling makes it a challenge to get to work on time in the morning for everyone (even rock stars). Desperate acts (like insider trading) to cover reckless behavior and frivolous spending are hallmarks of the avid partyer. These are not qualities of the esteemed chief executive officer.

2. Offshore corporate headquarters

When the company has the majority of its operations in the United States but holds one shareholder meeting every year in Bermuda (or the Cayman Islands or some other well-known tax shelter) in order to claim the island as its base of operations (and avoid paying taxes), you are dealing with a corporate ethos of rule bending. Another perk of this strategy is that it makes it extremely difficult for shareholders to attend annual meetings, especially "special" impromptu meetings. That means fewer inquisitive people are able to keep on top of what's going on with the corporation.

When someone has essentially unmonitored control over billions of dollars, you want that person to be a monk. However, the person who is attracted to helm a corporation that loves to bend rules to its favor is likely someone who likes to bend the favors toward herself.

Dennis Kozlowski went to prison, found guilty by a jury of his peers of stealing more than $100 million from Tyco International where he was CEO from 1992 to 2002. Tyco, which has 240,000 employees and conducts business in sixty countries, has home offices in Bermuda. Imagine how many shareholders were able to show up on a whim and hear the management's reasoning for the four-to-one reverse stock split at the Special General Meeting in March 2007.

This doesn't mean that you cannot ever make money on a company like this. Tyco has had a couple of run-ups in share price over the years. But the drop backs in 2002 and then again in July 2007, were *very* steep, and the company was trading lower in October 2007 than it had been ten years earlier. You can check out the home office address on the earnings reports and on the web site's investor relations page.

3. The SEC is conducting an investigation

Fewer than 5 percent of publicly traded companies are investigated in any one year, but you still want to take special note of those 5 percent. Nothing takes a company down faster than a scandal, especially if the Securities and Exchange Commission or the Manhattan district attorney files a lawsuit. You can Google the company name with the words "SEC investigation" or use "SEC" to do a keyword search in the company's earnings report. This *should* reveal anything that the company needs to disclose. Of course, an SEC investigation doesn't mean the company or the executives are guilty of a crime, but it could be a red flag, especially if you spot other suspicious signs in the company or eyebrow-raising reports about the chief executive. If the company later has charges filed against it, it could take a while for the share price to recover.

Imagine if all of the brainpower and a good deal of the manpower at the top have to be directed toward lawsuits or responding to demands from investigators, instead of improving the core products or services. The company could be eaten alive by the competition while executives are busy tidying up their house to please the regulators, even if the investigation reveals no foul play.

4. Confusing, complicated earnings reports

Are the company's quarterly reports harder to understand than quantum theory and the darkest caverns of your lover's brain? Or, like Enron, are they operating a dozen spin-off corporations with names you've never heard and employing complicated schemes that you don't understand? People who want you to understand what they're doing tell you in plain English and draw a flowchart if you still don't understand (much like Google does). When the executives behind the corporation are exciting investors with fantastic and hard-to-believe claims and then are refusing to answer journalists' hard questioning of the details, it's probably just one of the greatest stories ever told. This was another way you could have sniffed out the cooked earnings of divisions—like broadband in India—at Enron.

5. Product prices have sunk faster than the Titanic but earnings reflect steady growth

This was a hallmark of the telecommunications industry in the first part of 2000. Anyone with a phone was practically leaping for joy that they could now call anywhere in the United States for under five cents a minute. Wow! It was amazing. But at the same time that all of this revenue was disappearing from the top of balance sheets, many telecommunications companies were still releasing press statements touting "earnings growth." (Now you know: that was possible by over-billing and then having slow credit policies with some of the mega-wholesalers.)

In addition to using common sense to spot discrepancies in what the company is telling you about their earnings, you can check the debt-to-equity ratio to determine if the corporation is taking on more debt to fund operations. When there's an avalanche of income, as there was at Google and Apple in 2007, you're more likely to see very little or no debt in the corporation and a wad of cash and short-term investments.

6. Consensus insider selling

I've mentioned insider selling before, but there are a few more details to add. Most experienced executives—those that get hired to run huge corporations with market capitalizations in excess of $10 billion—know that they must exercise their stock options in a prede-termined plan. Bill Gates unloads about $500 million a year, largely to fund the Bill and Melinda Gates Foundation. For a man who owns 878 million shares, selling off sixteen million shares a year is not alarming. He's still got enough to last a lifetime (or fifty-five more years).

Where you'll see more problematic insider selling is with the rookies—young, smaller-cap corporations, as happened in 2005 with Intermix (then the parent company of MySpace). Insiders at Intermix were unloading millions of dollars at the time the company an-nounced an investigation by the New York prosecutor's office of the company's Spyware and Adware practices. (MySpace executives were not a part of the insider selling.)

Oftentimes, when the insiders of a young company dump their shares en masse, bad news is breathing down their neck. (It's against the law to trade on information that hasn't been made available to the general public, but tempting nonetheless.)

Sometimes you get lucky enough to spot insider buying, which can be a very good sign. Months before 1-800-CONTACTS was purchased by Johnson & Johnson, the insiders were buying their own company stock. When the acquisition went through, the share price quite naturally jumped, rewarding all stakeholders.

As a general rule, I wouldn't get too worried about insider selling by only one executive at a mega-cap corporation unless some of the other concerns outlined in this chapter are screaming at you. I would always consider insider selling to be a warning sign at any company with a market capitalization of under a billion dollars or if you see consensus insider selling by all of the top executives.

7. Delays

Delays in filing earnings. Delays in returning goods. Delays in adjusting credits. Delays in shipping. If it takes less time to swim to Antarctica than it does to receive a replacement part for your coffeemaker or to receive a credit on your bill for an unauthorized charge or returned item, these are big red flags. Delays in filing earnings reports are often a sign of increased scrutiny by an auditor, overly aggressive accounting policies, staff layoffs or other problems in the accounting office. None of those are good signs.

8. Bait and switch

When a company buys back shares of its stock or increases its dividends, that can be happy news for shareholders . . . unless it's a bait-and-switch tactic used to attract your attention while debt, earnings or liability questions are swept under the carpet. If you see analyst calls frequently being hosted by division heads (particularly sales) rather than the CEO and CFO, start sniffing around for what the company is not telling you. U.S. Airways isn't the only corporation to increase their share buyback program prior to going bankrupt. Corporate buybacks *can* be a sign that good things are happening at the company, and the board of directors wants the company to have a bigger piece of the upside. But experienced executives also know that money managers regard buybacks as a strong positive, and they use that to mask problems. You want to see increasing dividends *every quarter* over a period of years *and* increasing revenue to support the increased payout—in other words, consistency, not this quarter's dog-and-pony show. If you see other warning signs, but think you should disregard them simply because the company is buying back its own stock, think again!

9. Executive exodus

Captains may go down with the ship, but executives rarely do. Often, as was the case at Enron and was rampant within the airline industry post-9/11, division heads cash in and get out of Dodge, usually with the tag line that they "want to spend more time with the family." If two or more executives have jumped ship in the last few months, so should you!

10. Employees hate their jobs

The stores are filthy and under-stocked, and employees shrug off your questions. Rampant employee dissatisfaction is usually indicative of deep trouble within the corporation.

11. Muzak

Imagine the corporate malaise of a company that still plays Muzak (unless it's a joke). Steve Jobs drives his technical team nuts with his attention to detail. As a result, he has introduced some of the most amazing new products the world has ever seen. Do you remember Gateway's answer to the personal MP3 player? How about Microsoft's Zune? Thought so. Muzak is the antithesis of innovation, of cutting edge, of creating something customers can really get excited about using. Those who believe in conspiracy theories probably think that Muzak is played intentionally to kill our brain cells. Regardless of what's true, if I'm investing, I want my dollars to sponsor something cooler than a breezy rendition of Rage Against the Machine.

THE BOTTOM LINE

Almost all of the companies that have been spectacular performers for my e-zine are run by executives that I find inspiring, including eBay's former CEO Meg Whitman, Sohu's chairman and CEO Dr. Charles Zhang, Netgear's chairman and CEO Patrick Lo, U.S. Gold's chairman and CEO Rob McEwen, My Space CEO Chris DeWolfe and president Tom Anderson. I've interviewed most of these executives, and I can tell you personally that they are each hardworking, visionary, inspiring, honest men and women of integrity who have an easygoing laugh and long-term strategy. Each has a strong presence in the nonprofit community and a firm commitment to doing a great job for their employees, their shareholders and the world at large.

When you have a competent, inspiring, honest, hardworking CEO, the employees might be willing to walk through fire to create and deliver a product they're proud of. When the company is headed up by a narcissistic, dishonest, arrogant profligate, the "leaks" in the CEO personality could eventually sink the company's ship.

NATALIE'S THREE TAKEAWAY TIPS

1. Most companies that are publicly traded on Wall Street are not Enrons.
2. Freewheeling "rock star" CEOs who are often seen in the society pages partying with celebrities and are aggressive with their accounting policies (having offshore offices in tax-free countries like the Bahamas, the Cayman Islands, etc.) are, historically, more likely to be involved with a Wall Street scandal than their peers.
3. When the price of the company's core product falls dramatically, the corporation may be using accounting tricks to try to show revenue growth.

16

WAR, TERRORISM
AND ACTS OF GOD

When war ends, there is a very rapid recovery. As long as people retain the knowledge and skills they had before the war, there are good business opportunities directly after a war.
—Dr. Gary Becker

As one of the few people who tripled my stock investment in 2001 during a bear market year that saw the first strike on American soil since Pearl Harbor, I feel a bit qualified to talk about protecting your assets against war and terrorism. It wasn't easy. If I was the type of person who obsessed and worried about my money, I probably would have lost my investment, as so many people did.

On the fateful day of September 11, 2001, strangers all over the world were united in shock and horror. It was a day of horrific devastation. It was a day of unparalleled brotherhood. Firefighters drove from California to help their colleagues at Ground Zero.

Just one month earlier, in August 2001, I made a big stock purchase (for me). Two of my favorite companies, LoudCloud (now Opsware) and Genentech (DNA), were trading for very low share prices. I made the purchase and then focused on arranging for the care of my eleven-year-old son during a three-week business trip that I was scheduled to take. I had received a fellowship from the Virginia Center for the Creative Arts to finish a book I was writing, so, on September 10, 2001, I packed up my belongings and flew off to the artist's colony. The next morning, I awoke to the horror of 9/11.

Of course I heard, like everyone else, about the stock markets clos-
ing early and remaining closed for a few days, *but it didn't even register
with me*. I didn't even remember that I had purchased those stocks because I was so worried about making contact with my son and about
that rogue plane—the only one in the sky, which was reportedly
headed for LA. It took all day to ensure his safety while at the same
time trying to decipher what kind of threat was exploding just a few
miles up the road from me—in Washington, D.C.

When I began coming up for air a few weeks later, instead of focusing on the share price, which I knew was in the toilet, I focused on researching the movements of markets in the event of disaster. I
determined that I might have a selling window sometime between
three to six months after the inciting event, and I promised myself not
to even look at the share price until December.

I checked the prices in early December to see what kind of Christmas I could create. My stock was still beneath my buy price, but I was
so disgusted with all of the crappy gifts that I'd given my son over the
years that I went ahead and splurged for a paintball gun on credit card.

At the end of December when I looked at my share prices again,
the share price of Opsware had more than tripled and Genentech had
doubled. I hesitated long enough to double-check my buy price
against the trading price and then raced to the brokerage to sell the
stock. (My hands were shaking so severely that I worried I would hit
the wrong button when making the trade!) I was dancing on the ceiling of what felt like a graveyard at the brokerage. And, thank the
gods, I was able to easily pay for the gifts I'd bought my son. I was also
able to launch a financial news business.

It was a good thing that I sold my shares in December of 2001.
2002 was another down year in the markets. By fall, Opsware's share
price was trading for under forty cents, and the company was recon-
figuring itself to avoid bankruptcy.

CALM IN A CRISIS

Disasters in the stock market are opportunities to buy into companies that you've loved for a while but thought were out of your price range. So keep that shopping list of favorite stocks handy. And note that there's a big difference between buying into your favorite companies—that you prescreened before the disaster struck—and being seduced by the promise of hot tips that abound during disasters. As you can see below, most of the time, hot tips are money sinkholes. And for the socially conscious, your investing dollars, when others are panicked and jumping ship, could be just the thing to help your favorite company navigate over troubled waters—a win-win situation.

When you're tempted to watch television and act on any of the hot investing tips being touted by the so-called experts, please remember that, unfortunately, disasters really are the mother lode of news networks. Whenever there's a disaster, the cable networks and local stations provide valuable emergency information, but they also milk the misery for as long as possible simply because it earns a lot of money in advertising. Just think back to the death of Anna Nicole Smith or the coverage of Paris Hilton's time in jail (family tragedies, but not global events), both of which were passed off as news and trotted out at the top of the hour for weeks on end.

You don't have to rush out and buy into certain industries (say, defense) over others, although certainly some asset classes will always outperform others in specific scenarios. (The ongoing war in Iraq meant that millions of people had purchased defense stocks after the invasion, so they were no bargain between 2003 and 2007.)

You don't need to get your Ph.D. or learn how to read complicated charts or study up on your Nostradamus and astrology. In fact, continuing with your solid investment plan (meanwhile creating more peace in your own corner of the world) during war and acts of terrorism is largely a matter of common sense, acting according to a rationally laid plan and remaining calm, even while formerly rational people are at wit's end, screaming Apocalypse and making shoot-from-the-hip decisions.

From 2003 through 2007, despite the United States fighting a war in Iraq *and* Afghanistan, the U.S. markets enjoyed robust returns. In fact, the Dow pushed into record new highs in 2007. The volatility in the markets over that period was more directly linked with the high price of oil and the subprime mortgage loan implosion with little apparent impact from the daily bulletins on war casualties. (I'm sorry to say this—in honor of the young men and women who fought, were injured or died during those wars.)

The strategies I use to keep my own portfolio healthy in troubled times provide stability and a sense of confidence in good times as well. By preparing now, your nest egg will be in a stronger position if any act of terrorism, war or natural disaster should occur, so you can focus your energy on helping humanity.

NATURAL DISASTERS

Natural disasters are hard for the spirit and hard for the community, but they are never the Apocalypse (at least for the last few million years). That's why, if a natural disaster hits close to home, you focus on the human side and forget about your portfolio. If you've set things up right to begin with, you're going to be fine. If you haven't, you might be more vulnerable. But either way, you're better off making adjustments later, once you're calm and rational about the matter and the markets have had a chance to recover.

I just told you my personal story of investing in stocks shortly before 9/11, holding my positions and cashing out for impressive gains in December of 2001. Alternatively, I have a friend who told me that he lost over $35,000 after 9/11 (and that kind of loss wiped him out). When I asked him why he sold on September 14 (when the markets reopened), he shrugged and said that he'd been invested in a bunch of Internet stocks and that he would have lost everything anyway. I didn't have the heart to tell him that wasn't true. This friend did not have that kind of money to lose, and, in fact, he had to go to the hospital after 9/11 to get medication for heart palpitations (and he was under thirty at the time).

LoudCloud (now known as Opsware), the top performer in my 2001 portfolio, was a small-cap Internet stock. Opsware didn't bottom out (to a dismally low 39 cents) until a year later. Internet companies didn't just shutter the windows on 9/14 (not even the ones that had their offices destroyed in the World Trade Center). Many cleaned up, shored up and continued operating. And those that couldn't didn't give up until months after the attack. Thus, if my friend had waited to sell until late December or early January, after the Santa Rally, he might have recovered at least some of his investment and perhaps even made money (depending upon when he invested). The NASDAQ was up 30 percent in January 2002, after its low following 9/11. Blue chips had recovered 20 percent of their losses on average.

Portfolio Preparedness Tips

Below are more tips that you should get familiar with now—before disaster strikes.

1. Cash is king

Remember the rule of thumb that says you should always have six months of living expenses in liquid assets. Suze Orman makes a good point that you shouldn't put all of your cash in one long-term CD. Instead, she recommends that you stagger the maturity dates of multiple CDs so that you're never in a penalty position if you need to withdraw funds. The money market allocation in your brokerage account is another interest-bearing way of keeping cash on hand, as are treasury bills.

2. Make diversification your friend

Diversify. Diversify. Diversify. I've known as many would-be real estate moguls who lost it all by being all-in on real estate as I've known amped-up, bankrupt hedge fund managers.

Your best protection against terrorism and other natural disasters (including market corrections) is to not be over-concentrated in any one asset class—not real estate, stocks, bonds or backpack rockets. If you've never lived through an earthquake, fire, flood, riot or hurricane, trust me, these disasters can put you underwater on your mortgage faster than you can say Hurricane Katrina. Remember that *cash* is the best performing asset in all market corrections—natural disasters, wars and terrorist attacks. Gold is a good hedge against inflation, but is not as liquid as cash, so you might want to own some gold mining companies in addition to coins.

3. Check the small print on your insurance policy

Insurance is not necessarily your fix-all. In New Orleans, many people had their claims denied because flooding was not included on their insurance plans. The insurance companies argued that most of the damage was caused by the failed levies (flooding) rather than wind and rain associated with the hurricane (which was covered). Make sure you clearly understand exactly what your insurance covers *before* a natural disaster strikes.

Strategies for the Aftermath

If you're hit with an unexpected disaster, wait a few weeks before adjusting anything in your investment strategy. If you desire to buy into the stocks you have on your shopping list, wait a few days for the dust to settle and all of the panicked investors to sell and drive the prices lower and lower, before you purchase.

1. Don't panic—it's not the end of the world

The worst thing you can do as an investor is to sell everything because some doomsday prophet is scaring you into believing that the end is here. The U.S. economy isn't that fragile. Americans are resourceful, hardworking, imaginative, innovative, inventive, pull-together people—attracting the best and brightest minds to our soils since we first declared it the land of the free. If you panicked and sold after the 9/11 attack, you lost on average 35 percent for NASDAQ stocks and 17 percent for the Dow. People who had the foresight to *buy* when the markets opened—three days after the World Trade Center attacks—earned 30 percent on NASDAQ stocks and 20 percent on the S&P 500 and Dow Jones Industrial stocks within four short months (Figure 16.1).

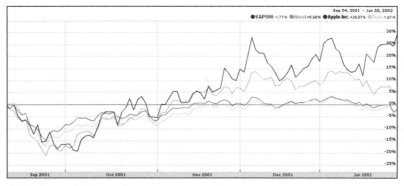

Figure 16.1. Stock Market Performance Sept. 4, 2001, through Jan. 30, 2002.
(Chart provided by Google Finance [finance.google.com].)

2. Buy on opportunity

NASDAQ reported 30 percent gains in just four months—by January 2002. During the same period, the Dow and S&P 500 were up 20 percent. This is another example of the "buy low, sell high" principle, and it works like a charm. So always have some extra liquidity in your portfolio during volatile times (war definitely qualifies) and keep a list handy of your favorite healthy stocks. (This can work well for real estate, too, providing you are buying stable, highly desirable land. I

wouldn't invest in New Orleans lowlands until I was extremely confident that the levies had been shored up.)

3. Don't buy anthrax or ebola remedies

In 2001, when there was a big anthrax scare, many investors rushed
out to buy one or another of the biotech companies that were reported to possibly have an anthrax vaccine. The first problem with this
"fools rush in" strategy: That's what everybody is doing, which means
that by the time your order is executed, the stock might be overpriced.
The second concern is that desperate people become over-jubilant
about marginal progress.

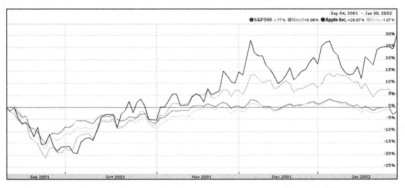

Figure 16.2. Human Genome Performance Jan. 3, 2000, through July 8, 2008.
(Chart provided by Google Finance [finance,google.com].)

Human Genome Sciences had an anthrax vaccine in Phase I trials
after 9/11. This is the earliest phase of human testing, the first of three
necessary phases, but investors (and television pundits) were leaping
for joy with their own (misguided) genius, thinking they'd found the
"miracle" cure for anthrax and that anthrax remedies were going to become as common as aspirin. Though the initial results for the vaccine
were "promising," everyone lost interest when the anthrax threat sud-
denly disappeared. Human Genome Sciences Inc. couldn't even get
funding to complete the studies. Human Genome Sciences was still

cash negative in 2007, having lost $243 million in 2005 and $240 million in 2006. Investors who bought in, for the most part, lost everything. (Figure 16.2)

4. *Consider cashing in gains at the first opportunity*

For the stocks in your Stocks on Steroids trading portfolio only, consider taking your profits at the earliest opportunity but after any short-term rally. (Recall that, historically, the Santa Rally will continue to post gains through the end of January.) If war or an act of terrorism causes a big hit to the economy, the fallout will show up more severely on earnings statements six to eighteen months out rather than in the one- to two-month, near-term statements. Investors who locked in some profits after the Santa Rally in 2001 were a lot happier than those who experienced 2002 all-in and had to go through a third straight year of losses in their portfolio and those who panicked and sold when the markets opened on September 14, 2001. (Figure 16.3)

Figure 16.3. Stock Market Performance Jan. 3, 2000, through Dec. 31, 2002. (Chart provided by Google Finance [finance,google.com].)

5. *Avoid hot tips*

In March 2003, at the onset of the Second Gulf War, Boots and Coots was the darling of the bulletin boards because they were expected to win a contract to put out oil fires in Iraq, as they'd done in

Kuwait during the First Gulf War. Boots and Coots did win the contract (as a subcontractor of Halliburton). Investors flocked in to buy the stock. But there weren't any fires to put out. Also, many investors didn't know how bad the company's balance sheets were and how much debt they owed. (There hadn't been many oil fires between the two Gulf Wars and thus very little revenue to the company.) Investors who bought into Boots and Coots at the high of ten bucks a share in February/March of 2003 have been burned for years on their investment. Boots and Coots was still trading at $1.65 in July 2007. (Figure 16.4)

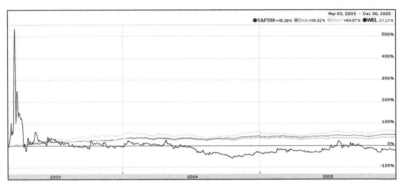

Figure 16.4. Stock Market Performance of Boots and Coots, March 3, 2003, through Dec. 3, 2005. (Chart provided by Google Finance [finance,google.com].)

6. Turn off the television

Watching disasters over and over again on television, with reporters covering every angle and interviewing anyone within a 400-mile radius, is not going to bring victims or your investments back to life. Healing your heart and your portfolio is going to take time. Wallowing in the horrific images over and over again brews up histrionics and can sway you into lousy decision-making—like buying high and selling low. The United States has certainly known wars, but between 1969 and 2006, through three wars and a major terrorist attack, the stock markets have still returned between 10.7 percent (large caps) and 12.8 percent (small caps) on average, every year.

7. Get help: Tax credits, FEMA and SBA

In natural disasters, there are many resources to get money to re-build or to reduce your overhead. If a natural or man-made disaster reduces the value of your home, petition to get a reassessment on the value of your property right away so that you pay property taxes on the lower value. This can save thousands of dollars. (The reassess-ment can be requested right away. Even if the appraisal doesn't occur for months, typically the new, lower value and property tax will be retroactive to the date of your request. Many homeowners don't know about this and simply miss out on the reduced property tax val-uation for years.) Check into tax credits, Small Business Administra-tion (SBA) loans and FEMA for any other government aid that you might qualify for. Get as much liquidity in your corner as quickly as possible to get you through the tough times.

The Federal Reserve Board of Governors devoted a section of their web site to distressed homeowners in 2007 during the subprime crisis. Believe it or not, the city, state and national governments do try to provide safety nets and incentives to help people get through tough times. (After the Northridge Earthquake, I used SBA loans and prop-erty tax reductions to help keep my family in our home. I'm living the American dream because I took advantage of government loans and grants—in addition to scholarships—for college.)

Notice, unfortunately, how focused these programs are on helping the homeowner, not the stock owner. There are not a lot of safety nets for the skittish stock owner who panics and sells her holdings for a loss.

THE BOTTOM LINE

Natural disasters, war and man-made calamities are part of our world, but that doesn't mean our economy is an engine of war and the best returns are made by capitalizing on death, destruction and mayhem. As you continue reading, you'll see that I believe peace = prosperity.

That bears out as more than just a philosophy. The Internet, software and clean energy companies I featured between 2002 and 2008 far outperformed the defense contractors—even though the United States has been at war since 2001. I have proven that you can invest in paperless offices, in freedom of speech (through the Internet media companies worldwide, even in China) and in renewable energy sources and still earn the highest performance record on Wall Street. Green is good for the world and for your wallet. Much better than war.

NATALIE'S THREE TAKEAWAY TIPS

1. Disasters in the stock market are opportunities to buy into companies that you've loved for a while, but thought were out of your price range. So keep that shopping list of favorite stocks handy.
2. There's a big difference between buying into your favorite companies—that you prescreen before disaster strikes—and being seduced by the promise of hot tips, like anthrax vaccines.
3. The average return for the stock market over the last twenty-five years through the end of 2007 was 12.4 percent according to Hulbert's Financial Digest. That time period includes many financial disasters, including 9/11, the Asian financial crisis of 1997, the U.S. debt crisis of 1992 and Black Monday 1987 when the Dow Jones Industrial Average dropped by 508 points.

---

1 7

THE TOP ELEVEN
INVESTING MISTAKES

I don't look to jump over 7-foot bars: I look around for 1-foot bars that I can step over.
—Warren Buffett

Investing mistakes are easy to make because doing what everyone else is doing feels like a time saver. Just follow the herd, no research or thought required. But the common mistakes you'll learn about in this chapter are not time savers at all. They're money losers, stomach-acid burners and sometimes even relationship deal breakers.

You'll find some people make a career of "contrarian investing," where they simply try to do the opposite of what everyone else is doing, thinking, "Aha! If these are the common investing mistakes, I'll just do the opposite!" It's a strategy that pays off—*only* when your crystal ball is working. However, reading a crystal ball is quite a trick! I'm not sure what skills are necessary to employ that kind of sixth sense, and I've watched a lot of contrarians make mistakes and lose a lot of money as a result.

Even if you know better than to fall into the pits of these common investing mistakes, you might still find yourself tempted to cut corners just to fit in with your peers or to save time. I'm including the rationale with each item on the list so that you've got an argument to use in case you need one with an overzealous friend, loved one or financial partner when they tell you—as it is likely that they will—to do something that you (now) know you shouldn't be doing.

MISTAKE # 1: FOLLOWING ANALYST RECOMMENDATIONS

If you thought Jack Grubman and Henry Blodget (the former analysts who got in trouble for recommending stocks in exchange for favors) were just flukes, guess again. Following analyst recommendations is a losing proposition. Researchers at the University of California and Stanford University found that, in the year 2000, the stocks most highly rated by analysts *lost* 31 percent for the year. Even more incredible is this finding from the study: The stocks *least* favored by the major analysts soared 49 percent. This study examined 40,000 stock recommendations from 213 brokerages. Analysts are not all crooks, but they are definitely not fortune-tellers.

Now, in all fairness, this is mostly just a case of supply and demand. When analysts say, "Buy," the brokers all buy (for their clients), and the share price goes up. When the analysts say, "Sell," the brokers all sell, and the price drops faster than soufflé. My Stock Report Card is designed to help **you** identify the leader in the sector *before* the analysts piece together the puzzle, which is a big reason the companies featured in my news e-zine have outperformed Wall Street.

MISTAKE #2: BANKRUPTCY BUYING

Think buying Delta at $1.54 a share is a brilliant idea because you're *positive* that they'll come out of bankruptcy and you just love flying on Delta's low-cost Song Airline? Guess again. Reorganization plans commonly call for the *cancellation* of the existing common stock with holders receiving nothing. *Nada*. (Translation: your stock becomes toilet paper.) Lawsuits are a difficult and costly way to try to recover losses.

MISTAKE #3: SCOOPING UP "PET ROCKS"

It's very tempting to buy stock after shareholders have earned seven thousand times their investment or after the product sells four gazillion copies, but that is chasing money (not making money). There were people, lots of them, who bought AOL Time Warner and Priceline at peak share prices in 2000 thinking that heavenly share prices could last forever. Too bad losing weight isn't as easy as losing money.

MISTAKE #4: CHASING HOT TIPS

Hot tips are often merely "pump and dump" schemes. Insiders pay marketers to *pump* up the stock so they can quickly *dump* when enough suckers fall for the charade and buy. These kinds of hot-tip scams abound with companies that are trading "off the boards"—the so-called penny stocks. Any hot tip you get for a company whose stock is selling for under $1 is likely to be trading off the boards and does not have to meet the same compliance requirements with GAAP accounting and SEC securities standards. Never respond to a direct mail or e-mail campaign to buy a stock *"Now,* before it explodes." No credible company would send a notice like that. The SEC has laws against solicitation of investments.

Assume hot tips are swampland in Florida unless proven otherwise by a gazillion independent, well-respected sources. Assume anyone who tells you that they have a "sure shot" that's going to double is lying, self-interested or, if it's a friend, maybe just gullible. Enron employees were giving out hot tips to their friends to buy stock at the April 2001 earnings report—which turned out to be a complete fraud.

MISTAKE #5: TAKING "SURE SHOTS"

Sure shots are slightly different from hot tips in that someone is assuring you that you will make a lot of money free and easy *right now* if you just do this or that investment trick. Time is always of the essence, as is secrecy, and you'll miss the opportunity if you insist on reading all the fine print. It might be "secured" third mortgages to distressed subprime borrowers. It might be a hedge fund run by someone who made 1000 percent gains last year. It might be an official trying to sneak money out of a corrupt country or a "lottery" you've won that requires your credit card number for shipping purposes.

Beware anytime someone wants you to hand over money before you have a chance to do proper due diligence. This includes lottery scams, Nigerian scams and other "phishing" ploys that are designed to capture access to your money and accounts. But it can also include second and third trust deed loans and other seemingly sound investment strategies. Any time you have money to invest, the grand ideas will start coming out of the woodwork.

There are a number of subprime mortgage buyers who are now blaming their mortgage brokers for selling them something they couldn't afford when, in fact, their signature is listed on pages and pages of disclaimers where the balloon payments and increased interest rates are calculated out. Most of us know that the real truth was that the sellers and the buyers were both doing business under the idea that the real estate market would continue to go up in value, as it had between 2000 and 2005. This was true of Internet stocks in 2001–2002. Don't be one of the blamers who complain when the tides turn on what was believed to have been a sure shot investment. Know what the average returns for the asset are over time and expect that any boom will also bust.

MISTAKE #6: PANICKING (OR SWOONING) OVER FRONT PAGE HEADLINES

Headlines are written by editors to catch your eye. If you don't read the fine print, you could be missing the most important information. Before United Airlines declared bankruptcy, investors gobbled up UAL shares on the headline that United had received $1 billion in promised concessions from its unions. The investors assumed that this was great news and that the labor concessions were all that United needed to soar into the skies once again and be profitable (with the help of some federal loans). A key consideration, however, was hidden on the inside pages of the article: the Federal Loan Guarantee required *$1.5 billion* in union labor concessions. In fact, receiving only $1 billion in concessions—when the loan was going to fall through unless $1.5 billion was delivered—was very *bad* news, not the good news that the headline trumpeted.

The loan guarantee application was rejected, and United Airlines was forced into Chapter 11 only a few weeks after that headline appeared in what many people consider the country's most reliable news source, the *New York Times*. The paper actually printed the important facts, but too many didn't take time to read beyond the headline (which was misleading). The headlines of less respected news sources can be even further from the complete story.

MISTAKE #7: FALLING FOR COMPANY HYPE

If you're researching online, you might come across a press release that looks fairly similar to a news report. However, press releases are written by professional writers employed by the company they are writing about, not by independent journalists. And press releases are not held to the same standards as the official corporate earnings statements that public companies must file with the Securities and Exchange Commission. A company can talk about an increase in revenue without ever mentioning that increased revenues don't mean the company is *profitable* or that, due to cash constraints, the company is about to declare bankruptcy. If you read anything that is from PRNewsWire or BusinessWire—services that distribute press releases written by corporate PR people—ask yourself, "What aren't they telling me?" Press releases can have valuable data and information, but they are designed to give you a snapshot of something newsworthy, not to draw the full picture.

MISTAKE #8: HAVING BLIND FAITH

Brokers are salesmen. They make their living by selling you real estate, mortgages, mutual funds and other investments. Many investors place far too much faith in their broker's knowledge, morals and information, when many brokers don't know the prognosis for the market they represent and are simply selling whatever product their company tells them to sell. You wouldn't marry a stranger, so don't hand your financial life over to one either!

MISTAKE #9: BETTING ON THE "HAIL MARY" INVESTMENT

Don't bet your livelihood on one Hail Mary investment! Diversify! Even with blue-chip stocks and prime real estate, you risk losing all of your money. Enron did go bankrupt, just one year after it was added to the *Forbes* Platinum 400 List, for revenue in excess of $100 billion. Real estate investors of 2005 were losing their homes in 2007. When you have your assets diversified across different investment classes—from real estate, to stocks, to bonds, to money markets, to treasury bills—you are protected against any one fluctuation or disaster. And in all instances, make sure that you keep enough cash on hand and enough income flowing in to meet your expenses and allow you to buy on opportunity when the rest of the marketplace is hurting.

MISTAKE #10: KEEPING TOO MUCH STOCK IN YOUR EMPLOYER'S COMPANY

ARISA guidelines state that you should have no more than 10 percent of stock in your own company. The majority of Enron employees wish that they'd known this. There's one exception to this rule: if you're the owner of the company, you may need a dominating percentage of the stock for voting/power reasons. In the early days of Apple Computer, Steve Jobs was booted out of the company he co-founded! Though it ultimately worked to his advantage—he became CEO of Pixar Animation, the most successful animation company of all time—try to avoid that, if possible!

MISTAKE #11: EMPLOYING FRIENDS AND LOVERS

I've spoken with women executives who have commanded billion-dollar corporations and others who have multimillion-dollar salaries who turned over their personal investment portfolios to a husband in order to make him feel "more manly." With men, it's more likely to be the guy at the country club who convinces his poker partners to come in on a sure shot investment of his.

Money means different things to different people, but, chances are high that whatever it means to you, it ranks in the red on your personal Richter scale and can cause personal devastation in high dosages when tremors occur. If your friend, loved one or relative loses your money, it's going to be hard to recover the relationship—no matter how much you like or love that person.

So, even though you might think it's an act of love to entrust your future to someone, it's potentially an act of annihilation. Somewhere down the road, that person can make a bad decision (in your eyes), or there will be less money than you hoped for (if any at all), or there will be a falling out between the two of you, or simply the person wasn't really qualified for that level of responsibility in the first place. Remember that selecting your financial partner is the second most important decision you make.

As Dr. Phil says, each partner in a relationship should have personal money that s/he can set on fire if s/he feels like it. Imagine how much more important it is for each partner in a relationship to control the life of her own dreams and the financial means to get there. I'm not encouraging you to hide money, merely steer your own ship in this regard. Have some personal passions fueling your short time on this planet, and use your Buy My Own Island Plan to help you get there. Whether you're a mother hoping for a better home for your children, a father preparing to send your kids to college, a bachelor building green skyscrapers or a nun building Habitat for Humanity homes, your desire for a better life can be your motivation to have more money of your own to invest and "play with."

Even if you hate investing, almost anyone can set up an auto-payment, tax-free, diversified retirement account through an online discount brokerage in just a few minutes. Take at least that amount of time.

THE BOTTOM LINE

Before your first child is born, it would be great to get a list of the Top Eleven Parenting Mistakes. Imagine how much easier it would be to know that the first time your child gets a scratch, you're likely to mistake it for a gash and spend a thousand dollars on a race to the ER. It's amazing how ridiculously easy the parent of four recognizes and avoids the common parenting mistakes and shakes her head knowingly at the rookie parents. The same is true of experienced investors. They know these tips like the back of their hand, and that is how they are scoring gains all up and down Wall Street on novices like you used to be.

NATALIE'S THREE TAKEAWAY TIPS

1. Turn off the news. If you're trading on headlines, you're late.
2. Ignore hot tips, sure shots, company hype, chasing returns and trading on analyst recommendations.
3. Distinguish between investigative financial news, press releases and smaller news organizations, which are mostly just reprinting the information found in press releases. Ask yourself, "What aren't they telling me?"

PART 4

Get Rich— and Stay Rich

(DON'T BE) FAMOUS AND BANKRUPT: THE FOOLPROOF GET RICH AND *STAY* RICH PLAN

Human prosperity does not abide long in the same place.
—HERODOTUS

Marion Jones, the superstar of the 2000 Olympics with a record five medals, made a fortune from endorsements. By mid-2007, she filed bankruptcy papers reportedly showing she was down to her last $2,000 "in total liquid assets throughout the world." Where did the money go? According to Ms. Jones, "Bills, attorney bills, a lot of different things to maintain the lifestyle."

Boxer Mike Tyson reportedly squandered over $300 million in lavish spending and by accepting bad advice. *Three hundred million!*

While most people become punch drunk on the idea of getting rich, the real trick is getting rich and *staying* rich. As athletes, Ms. Jones and Mr. Tyson have already passed their top-earning athletic years and will have a more difficult time making millions again.

The good news is that the solutions for getting rich and staying rich are the same. Many people who make millions overnight lose their money through lavish spending and bad financial advice. And a great many people who *could* become millionaires never do, through overspending and financial ignorance. (You'll notice a big difference between the modest lifestyle of Warren Buffett—a perennial billionaire on the *Forbes* list—and the lavish lifestyle of celebrities with a large entourage.)

What's the solution to getting rich and staying rich? The Thrive Budget and this book—financial literacy. You'll never go back to blind trust and frivolous spending ever again. Figuring out 10 percent of your take-home, limiting your basic needs to 50 percent of your income and adjusting everything accordingly doesn't require counting receipts or any extra time at all. Even if you think you can't add, you can drop a zero from your monthly income to come up with how much you should be spending on fun (10 percent short-term), on your best friend's new T-shirt business (10 percent on education or charity), etc. And because you'll enjoy blowing your fun money (which actually caps your "lavish spending" to a set amount each month), you won't even realize that your habits have now become a virtue and not a vice—part of your Thrive mentality, rather than your drowning in debt reality.

Now, there are a few other keys to getting rich and staying rich, which I've outlined below, but the budget and the literacy are the foundation.

GET RICH AND STAY RICH TIP #1: BE WARY OF
FAIR-WEATHER FRIENDS

You're going to have all kinds of new friends who claim to be aces at this or that investment strategy. Remember that it's ill-advised to take a huge lump sum out of one asset class, like equity from your home, and just dump it all in on another, like stocks. Likewise, don't take a loan out on your nest egg to invest in the new person's foolproof options software or solar technology. Stick to your long-term strategy. If you wish to "play," use your fun money. If you wish to invest, make sure that you own companies on Wall Street. Investing in a new business is not nest-egg investing. When you consider that there is about a 50 percent chance of the business failing within the first three years (higher in industries like restaurants, music and films), investing in startups is more akin to gambling.

GET RICH AND STAY RICH PLAN TIP #2:
THERE IS NO "BANK OF MOM"

Don't become the bank of the family. You're not qualified to, nor would you want to, establish the underwriting guidelines for loaning money to relatives. Nor would you wish to separate relatives into winners (because you anticipate a higher probability that they'll pay you back) and losers. And you certainly don't want to become the collection agency of the family.

When you are the one with the money, you're going to get hit up by everyone, and if you complain about it, you're just going to get talked about behind your back for being so cheap. Money-lending to family members is a lose-lose situation in most cases because they don't fully appreciate what you're giving them or what it takes to even earn that kind of money. And the odds that you'll get a lot of money back from someone who doesn't earn enough to pay back the loan is small.

So unless you're willing to make money-lending to the family your job and figure out the underwriting guidelines for that, it's best to not think of family money as an investment or a loan. With friends and family, if you do wish to let money change hands, it might be charity, or education, or even fun. Expecting a big gain on money you give to family is really silly, except in the rare event that the idea is sooooo awesome and the management team is sooooo adept that you're willing to set up a proper corporation and become a board director.

In this way, you'll keep a handle on the money that goes to relatives and friends and never have to say you're sorry that you did it. (You also have the excuse that you've already given to charity this month, if you wish to say no!) Even if you never see a dime in return, you'll still have received exactly what you desired from giving them money—a warm fuzzy feeling in your tummy if it was charity, or a degree if it was an investment in someone's education, or fun if you were just treating everyone to an African safari.

GET RICH AND STAY RICH TIP #3: TRADE TAX-FREE

Contribute the maximum amount into as many tax-free accounts as possible *every year.* If you're self-employed, you could qualify for larger annual contributions to SEP-IRAs. Ask about every IRA, college fund, health savings account, trust fund, endowment and foundation— every tax-sensitive tool imaginable—to enjoy tax-free wealth accumulation for you, your kids and the good of humanity. Tax-free accounts compound at a much higher rate than regular brokerage accounts that could give up a third or more of the gains to taxes. If you're really rich, the savings on taxes alone could add up to more money than you spend every year.

GET RICH AND STAY RICH PLAN TIP #4: BUY BONDS

It's much easier to buy bonds when you're a millionaire, and you're going to love the lower risk, combined with the steady yield. Your money manager should be able to help select a diversified portfolio of bonds for the safe part of your portfolio (that percentage that is equal to your age). Remember that bond *funds* are really stocks and are traded on the stock market, so don't simply invest in bond funds. In a bond fund, you're not buying a bond that comes to maturity and guarantees your principle.

GET RICH AND STAY RICH PLAN TIP #5: GAS UP

Fill up the tank regularly with biannual maintenance checks. Tithe monthly to your nest egg. Nurture it. Don't think that just because you're rich now, you don't have anything to worry about ever again. (Don't worry; simply employ sound strategies.) You may not always be earning the kind of income that you currently enjoy, so keeping the flow of funds in line with the strict (but delightful) guidelines of the Thrive Budget is key. Live, thrive and invest—within your means.

GET RICH AND STAY RICH PLAN TIP #6: GREAT EXPECTATIONS

Bonds are worth more when interest rates drop. When interest rates rise, the market value of the bond goes down and that can produce negative returns. So know the basic returns you can expect on the assets you hold so that you can sell high if they enjoy a run-up.

During 2002–2003, when bonds were the top-performing asset class at up to 25 percent gains, anyone holding a bond with a high yield (interest rate) was in a position to sell it for a good price over what they'd paid. ("High-yield" or "junk" bonds can return even higher rates of interest than the general marketplace because you are taking on higher risk by underwriting the debt of a company with a lower credit rating.)

A bond that goes to maturity is safe, provided you live long enough, but if you have any reason to believe that you'll not live to see the principle repaid, it's important to understand the relationship between interest rates and bond trading prices so that you price your buy and sell points accordingly. The same goes for real estate, stocks and other investments.

GET RICH AND STAY RICH PLAN TIP #7: HAVE SOME STOCKS ON STEROIDS

To really maximize returns, especially if you love investing in stocks and are willing to educate yourself and become a sophisticated, informed investor, designate a percentage of your stock portfolio as your higher-risk Stocks on Steroids account.

The percentage of your Stocks on Steroids portfolio should be in direct proportion to your experience and confidence in your own ability to pick great stocks and buy low, sell high for profit. A beginning investor might actively trade only 5 percent of their stock portfolio, whereas an experienced and young investor might actively trade half of their stock portfolio, provided they have the risk tolerance for it (and a lot of years ahead to earn more income). Remember that you're keeping a percent equal to your age safe—out of the market—at all times.

If you began with $4,000 and contributed $4,000 annually into a tax-free retirement plan and then used my NataliePace.com stock picks (assuming I maintain my 2006 record of 30+ percent annualized gains a year), it wouldn't take you thirty-one years to become a millionaire. You'd be a millionaire in just *fifteen* years. Imagine that!

GET RICH AND STAY RICH PLAN TIP #8: SWITCH HIT

Do your trading within your tax-free IRA, and use your non-qualified account as your long-term retirement plan. Oddly, even though the qualified tax-free retirement plan feels like the stodgy place you put money in regularly but don't bother looking at, the tax-free IRA is the best place to do your trading because the capital gains and dividends are not taxed.

A $10 million portfolio goes to half a *billion* in fifteen years with my 30 percent gains. But if you have to pay taxes on the gains at an average tax rate of 28 percent, that same $10 million invested the same way becomes only $187,933,000 in fifteen years. That's still rich enough to endow a building at your favorite university and have enough left over for the kids to inherit, but it's a long way from $500 million. Here's something to dream about tonight: What charities would you endow—what museums, what think tanks or medical research or environmental programs—if you had half a billion dollars? Imagine what the CEO of Exxon Mobil dreams about when the corporation is worth half a trillion dollars.

Because capital gains and dividends are not taxed in a qualified retirement account, you can really maximize your trading gains by housing your trading portfolio under that umbrella and avoiding those taxes. There are cap limits, so you can't just transfer your millions into an IRA and trade tax-free, nor can you dump in a bunch of existing stocks into your IRA. Consult your Certified Financial Planner for creative, tax-sensitive planning. If you have the millions to invest, they should have some great ideas for the best structure for you.

GET RICH AND STAY RICH PLAN TIP #9:
GETTY/GUGGENHEIM YOUR FAB SELF

Set up a foundation. Once you get into multimillionaire status, it actually pays to give back to your community. If you're smart about it, this foundation will not only earn great gains, but also benefit the segment of society that you most want to improve. (For Mike Milken it was cancer research; for Oprah it was education in Africa).

A foundation is also a great way to forge political alliances (important for anyone with money), a free way to generate good press and a wonderful strategy to earn gains within a more generous tax structure. The foundation will increase your net worth exponentially faster if you're investing well and have a good executive director managing the funds. Establishing your own foundation is a way of contributing to a society that benefits everyone, whereas just buying Rolls Royces for all your favorite relatives can be a short-lived thrill that you might even get taxed on at the extraordinarily high gift tax rate.

THE BOTTOM LINE

Wealth is not just money. Wealth is enjoying a happy, fulfilling enriched life with people you care about. So don't just create it, *keep it*, baby.

We wish Marion Jones well in her training and health and a return to success in her career and finances, but clearly her investment strategy is not the one to model. The better choice is to make sure you *stay rich* once you get rich. Once you know how to put your money to work and live the rich life in a balanced way, you'll be able to enjoy all that champagne, caviar and high life—without having to spend time in bankruptcy court explaining where all of the money went.

NATALIE'S THREE TAKEAWAY TIPS

1. Don't become the bank of the family. If you want to donate to your family and friends (or their businesses), consider that as part of your 10 percent tithe to charity, education or fun.
2. Start-up businesses are extremely high risk. Most fail—as many as 90 percent in some industries. New restaurants are much more likely to fail than new apartment buildings. Do not consider start-up investments in new entities to be a part of your "Buy My Own Island" plan. They are fun, charity or education.
3. Most people who make and lose millions spoil themselves and their friends ostentatiously and rely upon bad financial advice. Limit your basic needs expenditures, including attorneys, taxes and fancy lifestyle, to less than half of your annual income. Make sure that your financial advisor passes the test outlined in Chapter 9.

SURFING CHOPPY WATERS: THE ZEN BEAUTY OF MASTERY

When we choose our light, not our dark, our positive, not our negative, our good, not our bad, our peace, not our anger, our forgiveness and belief, not our blame or our shame, we are no longer at the effect of temporary circumstances.
—GARY KOBAT, LIFE AND FITNESS COACH TO THE STARS

Investing in the stock market for the first time can make you feel as vulnerable as you might feel surfing the North Shore of Oahu. And for the novice surfer and the naive day trader who race forward into the jaws of death with little more than an ankle strap, the chances that you're going to eat some sand are pretty high.

Wiping out hurts—a lot. But you're going to bite the dust less frequently if you take the time to master the smaller waves first. I've never lost much money on an investment, but I did have to endure those painful years of a sagging real estate market when my home mortgage was underwater. And I can tell you that even though the loan payments were less than rent would have been and the tax write-off was a great financial gain and the capital gain was good when I did sell it, having an asset that "lost money" on paper for a few years was **very** hard on my marriage. Since money is the primary problem in many marriages, learning the Zen art of wise investing—particularly if you educate yourself *with* your life partner—could really add a lot of feng shui to your home life. A nervous partner will be calmed by the confidence of watching the steady returns of your disciplined, experienced and masterful approach.

I live just a few blocks from the beach in Southern California, and both my son and I surf. One day, I found myself swooning as I watched the skill of a great surfer cutting up a ghetto Venice wave—which is more of a challenge to do something with than the gorgeously formed Hawaiian barrels. And then I realized that this is how I feel about my skill with investing. To me, even the harshest environments and most difficult opportunities are just another wave to master. And I understood at that moment that my life's goal was really to teach people tips on how to make investing that easy, so fluid, so second nature that it could be enjoyable—even Zen-like.

So many investors are nervous and uptight about money. Just as being nervous and uptight will make you rigid and easy to topple on your surfboard, so it is with the waves of investment opportunities. And if you've ever seen a surfer slip into a thundering tube and come out screaming victory on the other side, that's the orgasm you will feel the first time you double your money on an investment. The exact same hormone of victory is released!

You've stuck with me through this book, so you're not a novice anymore. Maybe you're not ready for the North Shore of Oahu . . .but you're surfing.

Most people are afraid of big waves simply because they've never even body-surfed a small one. Once you've mastered the basic skills, the waves become predictable, and your ability to lean in, catch a tube and then exit with flair sets you up to enjoy the heady pleasures of a healthy, exhilarating sport, even if you are just surfing ankle-slappers. What's frightening and even perhaps dangerous to neophytes is just sport to the master Zen surfer. Start small and increase your positions according to your experience and confidence level. Warren Buffett is plenty confident plunking down a few billion for a company these days. He started off small just like the rest of us.

If you can become a Zen-type investor, one who moves steadily and purposefully through your positions, you're more likely to become successful—and enjoy the process while you're at it. As you now know, the most common investing mistake people make is being jerked around by their emotions instead of being led by their skills and reason. Others wobble on their boards and topple over while you're ready to take a stand and carve your own signature atop the wave.

You don't want adrenalin, dopamine, panic or infatuation doing your investing for you. (Enjoy the rush of some of those hormones *after* you've sold for a profit.) So get comfortable, be willing to indulge in a little Zen mind-set and allow me some latitude for extending the surfing metaphor as I focus on the emotional part of investing.

PADDLE OUT ON A GOOD BOARD

I have to use a much bigger board than my son because I'm not yet as steady on my feet. In investing, don't just wing the math in your head (even the pros don't do that). Steady your emotions, even when you're pretty excited about a potential investment, by lining up the important data of the company *and* its competition in the Stock Report Card. For real estate, check out the historical resale values of homes in the neighborhood you're interested in buying into.

The foundation of any successful investment is simple: Will someone buy this from me tomorrow at a higher price? Check the history over the last few years, in particular the increase or decrease in sales and share price of the corporation or the trend of property value. Note any recent upticks or downturns that might signal the start of a new trend. Don't rely solely on reports that a company has "beaten earnings expectations" or that real estate in that area has been going up 20 percent every year. Don't listen to brokers who tout all the gains that have been made. Many brokers don't even know the historical performance of their industry, and this includes real estate brokers, stockbrokers, bond brokers and others.

Do the fundamental cash flow analysis yourself. Imagine who will buy the asset from you when you're ready to sell and why and at what price. Make sure that the fundamentals of your investment are steady and sound.

SWIM SIDEWAYS ACROSS RIPTIDES

Swimming frantically for shore against a riptide is the worst thing to do. Likewise, selling in a panic on a piece of bad news is portfolio suicide. A lot of money has been lost by panicking. Patience and profits are better P words.

GO UNDERWATER AND WAIT IT OUT WHEN THE WAVE CRASHES OVER YOUR HEAD

Even the most skilled surfer has a few wipeouts, so don't worry if one or two companies in your portfolio head south for a while on bad news. Trust your investment strategy, just as a great surfer trusts her abilities on the waves. Rely on fundamentals, not hot tips or headlines. Sometimes the marketplace has the jitters irrationally over an investment that is fundamentally sound and attractive. If you've done your research beforehand, you'll feel more confident riding through the storms.

However, if all your stocks are doing miserably, then your research criteria might be diseased. (Conversely, if all your stocks have been winners in the last three years, you're ready to write a book . . .) If you need some stock market strategies that work, find that stock guru who has been performing strongly for a good number of years and simply mimic her moves until you can surf Wall Street on your own.

HAVE PATIENCE: THE TIDES ALWAYS TURN

Some years, Internet stocks are all the rage. Other years, it's real estate. Sometimes clean energy. Investments run in cycles. If you're at the top of one, take profits. If you're at the bottom of another, buy in. As you come to understand the waves of investing, you'll become more secure with your drop-in and cash-out points.

Economic growth and expectation for return on investment in most asset classes (real estate, stocks and bonds) began to moderate in 2006–2007, with a lot of volatility, however, which enables people who trade actively to eke out greater returns by "trading around the core" (a technique of many professional traders that involves buying a favorite stock on bad news and selling on good, usually for smaller, incremental returns.) Make sure you factor in the tax consequences of short-term gains before engaging in this strategy. Typically, there's one company that begins to catch speed and momentum at the expense of the other competitors and one industry that heats up faster than other investment classes.

Be poised for the waves of opportunity. Liquidity (cash on hand) helps. When stocks are hot, real estate might be cool. When stocks tank and real estate rallies, other sectors, like copper, lumber, concrete and other building materials might soar as well.

THE SEVENTH WAVE IS USUALLY WORTH WAITING FOR

Surfers know that a series of short waves come before the monster wave. Investors learn to know the seasons of the markets and how to be patient for the right buy and sell price. Be suited up, on your board, in the water, with liquidity and your stock shopping list, ready for the investment opportunity, just as surfers are for that magic "seventh wave."

When you have your stock shopping list at hand and have the patience to watch for a "buying opportunity," that is the way to secure the greatest gains. I keep a running list of the companies that I report on in my online stock e-zine. When they are expensive, I keep reporting until they've had their run and it's time to take the company off of the list. I highlight great stocks when they come into attractive buying range.

DRAG YOUR FEET IN THE SAND—IT SCARES OFF THE STINGRAYS

If your broker (or anyone else) is pushing you hard to do something fast, slow everything down. End the meeting if need be (make an excuse that you have to pick up your sick kid from school or something) and schedule another one for another day. Ask the hard questions, even if you think they are so ridiculously silly that you will sound like a complete idiot. Don't get bullied into believing that you need to act *right now* or you'll miss out. If you're sitting in front of someone who bullies you every time you ask a question, you're definitely working with the wrong person.

The same holds true of real estate and mortgage brokers. They had a field day between 2000 and 2005. By 2006, many sensed that rising interest rates, tighter lending policies and sky-high prices (in many regions of the United States) meant that fewer people would step forward to buy, and fewer buyers would qualify for a loan. Don't be suckered into a bad buy decision by an aggressive salesperson who **needs** your commission to pay her own home mortgage or office rent. Remember, the truth is that stocks outperform real estate over the long-term. And it is simply a lie that more money has been lost in the stock market than real estate. Ask the Japanese who bought Rockefeller Center in the 1980s.

Consider carefully before pulling *any* equity out of your home to invest in the stock market, even if someone is telling you that is the way to pay the piper for the variable interest rates or the balloon payment you're stuck with on your home equity loan. Sound investment strategies are based upon setting aside a portion of your *income*— money you earn on the job not a portion, or all of, the home you live in. As a general rule, you don't want to get fancy or risky with where you lay your head to sleep at night!

WHEN THE WAVES GET TOO BIG, WATCH THE PROS FROM THE SHORE

Let's face it: If the waves are tsunamis, the best strategy isn't grabbing a board and racing into death. It's a much better idea to practice on the two-footers first. Watch (and read up on) how the pros do it. Get to know the trends of your favorite stocks by trading in a mock setting before you place your money on the line. (Many online brokerages and financial sites offer easy fictitious trading accounts to do this in.) And know where the average P/E for the marketplace is or the average prices of the local real estate market, especially if you are considering making a big move all at once.

How do you know if the waves are too big? Check your pulse. If you're investing more than you can stomach, the waves are too big. If you're placing a buy order for an individual stock that will cost you more than you're willing to lose, your position is too big. Investing success rides on a long-term strategy of steady deposits, reliable gains, compounding, diversifying and profit-taking—not a roller-coaster ride.

But this doesn't mean you have to leave the beach altogether. For your long-term portfolio, the strategy is different. Even if the waves are crashing a few feet out from shore, you can still dip in your toes safely from the sand. Don't wait to start tithing monthly to your Freedom Plan, thinking you can find a better time. For the safe part of your portfolio, the sooner you get started, the better, regardless of market conditions, especially if you're young. Over time, the buys in your long-term portfolio will all average out because some years you're buying in on the low side, in some higher.

WEAR A LEASH, SO YOU'RE NOT ALWAYS CHASING YOUR SURFBOARD

Have a sell strategy, especially in your Stocks on Steroids portfolio, but also in your Buy My Own Island Plan. Don't watch your gains drift out to sea. The tides always turn, whether in real estate, stocks or any individual investment. Have enough cash on hand—and a strategy that includes evaluating opportune buy and sell prices—so that you can buy when you want to buy, sell when you're getting the best price and laugh all the way to the bank.

DON'T FORGET THE SUNBLOCK

What's the best strategy for not getting burned on investments? Slathering information all over your beautiful brain. Is the product hot? Are the company products winning awards and flying off the shelves? Are sales increasing? Is this the best company or real estate in its sector? Are you buying at top dollar when you should be paying a more reasonable price? Buy-and-hold works for the long-term horizon. "Buy low, sell high" works every time.

THE EARLY BOARD CATCHES THE BEST WAVE

If you're very confident about a stock and the buy-in price or some undervalued real estate in an emerging area, don't wait for the rest of the world to agree with you. Catch the wave at dawn, while everyone else is sleeping. (Do, however, make sure that the information you're basing your judgment on is accurate.) Once the word gets out, let investors compete to buy your shares or your property and drive up the selling price.

When banking on something that others don't yet believe in, it pays to be the expert in that arena. Bill Gates, the chairman and founder of Microsoft, got into software before people could even imagine that every person in the developed world would own a personal computer. The Google founders, Larry Page and Sergei Brin, were perfecting their Internet search engine's functionality when "tech" was still a four-letter word on Wall Street (after the Internet crash in 2000). Sheldon Adelson, the CEO of the Las Vegas Sands Corp. (owners of, among others, the Venetian Resort Hotel and Casino), was the first to believe that there was a way to attract hordes to Las Vegas during the week: develop a strong convention market. He was also the first "outsider" to open a casino in Macao, now called China's Las Vegas.

THE BOTTOM LINE

Teachers often say, "Practice makes perfect." You will become a much better investor if you get in the water on a regular basis and practice the skills outlined throughout this book. When I graduated from the University of Southern California with my degree in English Literature, I certainly would have laughed if anyone had suggested that I'd be ranked as the top stock picker in the United States. But I read a lot more earnings reports these days than I read books.

If I can do that, you can certainly surprise yourself with how great an investor you can become by riding the wave of your own passions and intellect. I've heard the delightful reports of too many satisfied subscribers to believe otherwise.

Namaste.

NATALIE'S THREE TAKEAWAY TIPS

1. Limit the amount of your "trading" portfolio to your level of experience. If you have never traded a stock before, start with a fictitious portfolio, which many discount brokerages and web sites offer online. Even if you are an experienced, successful trader, you should not be subjecting your entire nest egg to the risk associated with trading individual stocks.
2. Have a sell strategy.
3. Panicking on a piece of bad news is portfolio suicide. Patience and profits are better P words.

HAPPY PEOPLE MAKE BETTER PRODUCTS FASTER, CHEAPER: MY THEORY OF ECONOMIC EVOLUTION

Things are never as complicated as they seem. It is only our arrogance that prompts us to find unnecessarily complicated answers to simple problems.
—MUHAMMAD YUNUS, 2006 WINNER OF THE NOBEL PEACE PRIZE, FOUNDER AND MANAGING DIRECTOR OF GRAMEEN BANK AND BEST-SELLING AUTHOR OF *Banker to the Poor* AND *Creating a World Without Poverty*

Many people have asked me to reveal my secrets to finding the leader in the sector—that company that is poised to lead the pack, to break out of the current growth trend and shine in product sales and share-price growth. Typically, I try to keep my writing focused on simple "recipes for the rich life," through easy-to-understand and easy-to-use strategies that will jump-start your prosperity. In this final chapter, I am going to talk about a more sophisticated hypothesis that I have been employing for years. It's not that difficult to understand, and now that you know how to factor this type of underreported yet valuable information into your investment strategy, I trust you'll find it useful.

It all began on the back of a cocktail napkin at one of the first women's conferences where I was asked to speak, in New York City, back in 2004. I was at dinner with a handful of very intelligent, delightful, candid, colorful and successful women who were going to be speaking on the panel with me the following day. We were chatting about the upcoming election in Afghanistan, where women were risking their lives to vote for the first time in history. At the time, I wasn't as well-read in economic theory as I was in street economics, but I'd had some noteworthy success in picking stocks and identifying market trends. I had also formed some strong opinions as to what inspires someone to work hard and what gets someone mad enough to risk her life in defiance. (Having run away from home—the first time—at the age of twelve, essentially risking my own life to trek from a small town in Arizona to Los Angeles, I understood very personally what kind of pressures exist to motivate someone to do that.)

I called this napkin masterpiece my Theory of Economic Evolution. Thankfully, one of the women at the table, who is now a business advisor, was enthusiastic about the idea and encouraged me to write the theory out in detail.

My Theory of Economic Evolution is based on a simple time line, assuming that the person already has provided for basic needs like health and housing.

The Economic Evolution Timeline:
1. The right to vote
2. The right to get any job
3. The right to will your estate

According to this theory, the *a priori* tendency toward not just freedom, but economic freedom, is so fundamental to an individual that virtually everything from war and peace, revolution and civil disobedience (such as gang warfare), to divorce rates and employee productivity, can be predicted based on this fundamental model of social evolution—the economics of freedom. While a country, or a company or even a marriage is advancing along nicely on the evolutionary time line (which is essentially a path toward greater personal freedom of the individual), the citizens, employees or marital partners have more tranquility, so the ground for prosperity and productivity is rich. Conversely, when a subset of the population, whether it be citizens, employees or a marital partner, feels trapped and stifled in their rights to economic freedom, the seeds for contention are sown and the ground is ripe for chaos, war, strikes, divorce, suicide and other unproductive uses of time (arguing, complaining and the like).

Common sense tells you that happy people make better products faster and cheaper than depressed people, so the country, corporation or marriage that paves the path for personal freedoms is the country, corporation or marriage that experiences greater sustained prosperity. Common sense and observations of human behavior also tell you that unhappy people throw a wrench in the works. Civil disobedience, union strikes, marital strife, civil war and more occur when individuals are no longer engaged and "invested" in the success of the social structure. The theory of economic evolution suggests that the most fundamental way of keeping individuals invested in the success of the country, company or marriage is to satisfy an innate longing for personal economic freedom and to anticipate just when they will be desiring the next level.

Now, this is a case of progress forward being more important than arriving; that is, the journey up the road toward greater freedom is what is important. Whenever a person feels that s/he is being denied or losing freedoms that s/he has a right to, that person is likely to engage in unproductive behaviors. But as long as s/he feels more free today than yesterday and believes s/he will feel still freer tomorrow, even if s/he is less free than someone on the other side of the world, s/he is likely to have a spark in her step and work productively toward the greater success of the social structure (and more freedom for herself and her countrymen).

A twenty-year-old may not see far enough into her future to care if the government or her employer is providing a retirement plan or a health care package, but is keenly interested in career advancement now. The twenty-year-old recently got the right to vote and is now looking to get a better job. The forward-thinking company, knowing that the individual *will care* about willing her estate in the future, should pave the path for continued prosperity, possibly by offering a 401(k) to individuals after a certain period of employment. On the other hand, a sixty-year-old may make career choices based *solely* on matters of the estate. She has had the right to vote for years and is looking forward to retirement, not career advancement. Thus, how well a company, a marriage or a country "frees up" the rights of its citizens to stride forward on the evolutionary path to greater economic freedom is one of the most reliable measures of peace, productivity and wealth.

My own limited point of view serves also to illustrate how the model works. Even though I've got my dream job and have learned to will my own estate, I cannot yet see what lies beyond the economic freedom of willing one's own estate. (Death?) In this evolutionary model, it's presumed that the progression of "freedom" marches beyond this milestone, even if I don't know what that milestone is—yet.

Imagine then, how a slave or a servant (or a woman living in Afghanistan) may not see far enough into the future to imagine owning her own plantation or becoming a doctor but is willing to risk her life for the right to vote. Likewise a young assistant may not be overly concerned about the 401(k) but is highly motivated to get a raise and a promotion. As one steps along the path to economic freedom, one sees the next plateau to attain. As long as one is moving forward, the perception is freedom, which is an "engaged" state of being, highly productive and invested in the outcome and continued success of the societal structure (government, corporate or marital). This personal feeling of empowerment, of having all restraints on personal prosperity and potential stripped away is both powerful and productive and not as difficult to employ in practice as you might imagine. (Muhammad Yunus and Grameen Bank have done a brilliant job of structuring incentives for women who are lifting themselves out of poverty. Read *Banker to the Poor* to learn more.)

The United States is, by my calculations, about midway between the right to vote and the right to will one's own estate, depending upon which neighborhood you live in. The United States is well advanced on the time line in economic rights in the legal sense, but not in practice. Blacks had the right to vote for 100 years before they could really exercise the right to shape the larger social structure; they were still forced to segregate themselves as late as the 1960s. Today, though discrimination in employment is illegal, high schools in poor communities experience the highest dropout rates—which limits the ability to secure the best-paying jobs.

Not surprisingly, the poorest neighborhoods with the highest dropout rates also have higher crime rates, which is consistent with this economic evolutionary theory. Many poor U.S. communities are stuck between the right to vote and the right to get any job. Some ethnic groups are very good at quickly advancing economic freedoms by placing education as a priority, which explains why these groups are also quick to assimilate and prosper in the larger community.

In August of 2007, the Census Bureau issued a press release with a startling statistic: Asians, which were formerly considered one of the underserved minority groups in the United States, are now the top earners. According to the Census Bureau press release, "Asian households had the highest median income at $64,200, followed by non-Hispanic white ($52,400), Hispanic ($37,800) and Black ($32,000) households."

Similarly, women have had more freedom on paper than in practice in the United States, at least until very recently. Women won the right to vote less than ninety years ago, but as late as the 1970s, no woman was the head of any Fortune 500 company that she didn't inherit. (Christy Hefner was one of the first female presidents in the United States as the president of Playboy, her father's company.) One of the most celebrated tennis players of all time, Billie Jean King, couldn't get a sports scholarship to attend college. Supreme Court Justice Sandra Day O'Connor was offered secretarial positions after graduating at the top of her class at Stanford Law School. In 2006, women accounted for only 13 percent of board directors, only 15.7 percent of corporate officers and women of color held only 1.6 percent of C-level spots (CEO, CFO).

The limitation on jobs available to women is rapidly disappearing today. One-half of law students and medical students and one-third of MBA candidates were women in 2007. And as women are earning their own money in any job they desire, they are also taking charge of their investments. In more traditional, older couples, men are still more likely to manage the nest egg, but young professional women are getting great jobs, buying their own homes and entering relationships with their own retirement plan. If the Theory of Economic Evolution is accurate, that kind of individual freedom is great for marriages, not threatening.

I would love to see more research on the number of divorced, separated or abandoned mothers living in poverty, as opposed to the number of divorced, separated or abandoned professional mothers. (Single mothers make up the largest group of people living in poverty in the United States by far.) My suspicion is that there is a strong negative correlation between financial freedom and divorce. If there is a correlation between personal economic freedom and happiness, then I'd expect to see that the divorce, separation and abandonment rate is much higher for mothers living in poverty than it is for professional mothers.

And that is indeed what Dr. Muhammad Yunus, the founder of Grameen Bank, reports. Grameen Bank opened in Bangladesh in 1976 at a time when only 1 percent of the borrowers in the country were women. Today, Grameen Bank serves 7.5 million borrowers, 97 percent are women. Over 600,000 of these women own their own homes, and many earn more than their husbands—in an Islamic culture.

At the California Women's Conference in Long Beach, California, in 2007, Professor Yunus said:

> Divorce is such a common thing among poor people [in Bangladesh]. You just say I divorce you three times and it's done. Very simple. But within these 600,000 houses, that doesn't take place because the husband knows very well that no matter how mad he gets, if he says that, he's the one who has to pack up and go.

The Theory of Economic Evolution might explain why freedom, opportunity and education are correlatives of productivity, which is in turn a key predictor of economic growth. Education is fundamental to getting any job you want and to learning how to will your own estate.

HOW THIS RELATES TO INVESTING

I do not intend to suggest here that this brief explanation of how the model works in theory is proof of anything or is a panacea for all of the world's problems. It's just one way of thinking that has helped me to identify countries and companies that are poised for robust economic growth, and which, as a result, experience more prosperity and productivity than their peers. Those companies and countries that have motivated, happy, productive stakeholders tend to be breakouts—which is largely responsible for my success as a stock picker. Companies that know how to motivate their employees and get them to work hard and smart for the benefit of the corporation are going to have a competitive edge over their peers.

As another illustration of how this theory works in real life, check out the explosion of economic growth that has occurred in Eastern Europe and China. Eastern Europe was formerly a region devastated by civil war, under Communist rule. China is a Communist country that has only recently, and aggressively, moved to a (more) free economy.

Eastern Europe has a very high concentration of well-educated persons. Over the last few years, many Eastern European countries have been aggressive about advancing personal freedom to own property and about establishing pro-business policies. As a result, Estonia, the Czech Republic and Lithuania were all ranked in the twenty-five most economically "free" countries in the world in 2007, according to the Heritage Foundation and *The Wall Street Journal*. As we see in the chart below, the GDP growth rate of these Eastern European countries was on the high end of the world's countries, double that of their Western European counterparts.

EUROPEAN GDP GROWTH RATE
COMPARED TO FREEDOM

Country	GDP Growth Rate (in 2004)	Freedom Ranking
Estonia	7.8 percent	12
The Czech Republic	4.7 percent	31
Lithuania	7 percent	22
France	2.1 percent	45
Germany	1.6 percent	19

Source: *2007 Index of Economic Freedom*

While Eastern European countries are rebuilding and enjoying an infusion of capital and prosperity, Western Europe is experiencing more panic, public insurgencies and violence. The headline story in the *New York Times* on March 29, 2006, was "French Protests Turn Violent." Why were rioters demonstrating? The people felt their workplace rights were being taken away.

On March 28, 2006, the workers walked out; even the Eiffel Tower was closed. French newspapers were printed but not distributed. Mail was not delivered. The Paris National Opera canceled its ballet performances. More than a million people left their jobs and stormed the streets (labor unions claimed it was up to 3 million) to protest a law that was passed by the legislature and approved by Prime Minister Dominique de Villepin that allowed employers to dismiss workers who are under the age of twenty-six "without cause" during the first two years of employment.

Parisians were willing to shut down their city in protest, which is ironic because the only way a nation can be prosperous is if the citizens work together (not protest together). On the other hand, the future and job possibilities in the former nationalized Eastern European countries have never been better, and productivity is, as a result, booming. The people of Eastern Europe are just a few years beyond war, upheaval and a highly regulated economy and existence and are highly motivated to rebuild a better country for themselves and their children.

Now, *The Index of Economic Freedom* ranks countries by the amount of freedom *currently allowed* in business and property rights, whereas the Theory of Economic Evolution places more value on how well the country is removing impediments to progress *toward* greater personal economic freedom. According to the *2008 Index of Economic Freedom*, Germany ranks 23rd in terms of free economy, while China qualifies as 126th out of 157 countries. Yet China's Gross Domestic Product growth rate was 10.4 percent (in 2005), the highest in the world, double that of most countries in Eastern Europe and far superior to Germany's stalled 0.9 percent GDP growth rate. (India is another country that ranks low, number 115, on the Freedom Index, but is making huge strides toward economic freedom of the corporation and individual, experienced 9.2 percent GDP growth in 2005.)

What gives? China may not have great freedoms by Western standards, but the growth of personal freedoms on their own economic evolutionary time line is outstanding. This formerly Communist country is actively promoting personal enterprise at an unprecedented rate, and thus the optimism of the inhabitants is high, as is productivity and growth. People are migrating into the cities en masse and opening up new businesses like mad. It's hard to imagine that the student-led Tiananmen Square revolt (and massacre) calling for democratic reforms was in 1989, less than twenty years ago.

China, Eastern Europe and India are great examples of the way that robust "forward movement" in economic freedom is a better predictor of GDP growth than a state of freedom that is advanced but static (or declining).

Is there any way to keep productivity high during a recession (or other challenging period of readjustment in the already free society)? A society, corporation (or marriage) is extremely vulnerable during hard times because the individuals are likely to experience stagnation or backsliding of their personal prosperity and freedom. Unless everyone buckles down and works together as a group, and no one feels worse off or picked on than those around them, there are likely to be riots, dissension and chaos. Thus the leader with a message of hope might convey that no one will be stripped of rights, and everyone, including the "higher ups," will share in the sacrifices and hard work necessary to promote prosperity. Think of King Henry the Fifth's famous Agincourt speech, and that is an example of how a leader might rally the troops under the worst possible conditions to win the battle.

THE BOTTOM LINE

In short, the *perception* of freedom must not wane. Thus, the corporation whose leaders take a salary cut when their workers are taking one should be more popular than those who pad their golden parachute even as they shuffle employee pension plans over to the U.S. government. In fact, American Airlines CEO Donald J. Carty was forced to resign after it was discovered that he had negotiated wage and benefit concessions from the unions at the same time he was planning to pad some executive's compensation packages. CEOs are the soul of their companies, and how they structure the business and compensate, empower, reward and acknowledge their employees is a key factor in success.

The Theory of Economic Evolution proposes that when people are happy at work and happy with their lives, there's no motivation or desire to mess that up. The better the system is working for them, the better they work for the system. Again, happy people make better products faster, cheaper. This is something you can see and feel every time you walk into a store, or up to an airport ticket counter, or when you speak to a customer service representative. Factor it into the mix when you're evaluating the leading company in a sector. A company (and a nation) is only as good as the productivity of the people it employs.

NATALIE'S THREE TAKEAWAY TIPS

1. If the product you love is priced right and fresh at your fingertips, one thousand things have gone right—from the executive suite to the factory to the salesman to the store. On the other end, if you see disgruntled employees and slipping product quality, those are signs of deeper trouble at the core of the company and investment.

2. Companies that stay proactive about empowering the individual and promoting healthful working conditions have a competitive edge over bureaucratic, stodgy corporations.

3. International investing is not as simple as investing in the countries that are perceived to be the most "free." Even less "free" countries, like India and China, can experience robust economic growth when their citizens are motivated to achieve and succeed.

THE PATH TO WISDOM

Investing is like learning a foreign language. When you start out, it looks and sounds like gobbledygook. As you learn to understand the gobbledygook, you start recognizing patterns and piecing together a few broken phrases. Before you know it, you're translating whole sentences of this new language—P/E, D/E, GDP and strange theories of economic evolution—to your friends. As you master this new world, you may even—like Sergey Brin and Larry Page, the founders of Google did—find yourself inventing new words!

There's no shortcut to wisdom, only walking forward, educating yourself and practicing with the new tools that you're given. You cannot look at the symbols from Japanese pictographs, jet straight to understanding what they mean and then become a master at haiku in minutes.

Technical analysis software is no substitute for the path to wisdom. It's trying to predict the future with data from the past. In market parlance, that's like driving while looking in the rearview mirror—an easy way to crash.

So love your money, exercise sound fiscal habits, tithe and you'll create such a healthy nest egg that you'll never need a financial surgeon. Remember—with the stock market returning 11 percent over the last twenty-five years, it has been healthier than real estate, bonds and euros, despite the occasional highly publicized flu season.

If you were diagnosed with high blood pressure, which would be more effective: taking your blood pressure every day and fretting about all of the diseases you might fall prone to or exercising and eating right? Chances are that you're already invested in the stock market, so isn't it better to employ healthy fiscal habits and build a healthy portfolio than it is to panic over headlines? Haven't you noticed that most "news" is simply bad news or gossip?

You wouldn't expect your doctor to exercise or eat right for you, and you shouldn't expect your financial planner to be watching meticulously and carefully over your nest egg—while s/he does the same for her 400 other clients simultaneously. Fiscal health has a lot to do with your healthy money habits and choices. Getting rich and staying rich isn't about giving up control and trusting blindly. The key is in getting smarter about *everything* that has to do with your money, including how to select an honest and successful money manager and how to set up a budget that launches you out of basic needs and into the land where dreams come true. It requires less time, really, than all the time and energy people waste complaining, worrying and arguing about money.

Educating yourself means that you become a better partner with your broker. If you're always yanking her around based upon market fever, you're going to be a hindrance to great gains, even if your financial planner is a smart and honest one.

There are many people, especially in free countries like the United States, who have proven that *when you make love with your money, you live a rich life and you enrich our world*. Join us.

Life is not a war. It's a play.

Yours in peace, health, happiness and prosperity. (Yes, you *can* have it all.)

                                    —*Natalie*

APPENDIX: FREE INVESTMENT CLUB STARTUP KIT

Go to NataliePace.com and click on the Investment Club Startup Kit banner ad to get your free Startup Kit.

ACKNOWLEDGMENTS

NATALIE PACE

I just took a leadership test and discovered that I'm not much of a nurturer. Expressing thanks is not something I'm very good at, and I'm sure this part of the book is going to be more difficult than the 70,000+-word draft that I initially wrote (which Bill Simon got to weave into something far more organized than it was when it landed on his desk). I'll probably forget someone who is really important to me. I am so blessed and rich in friends, family and business associates that a real acknowledgment and thanks would be a book in and of itself.

First, I have to thank Marilyn Tam for introducing me to Bill Gladstone, and Bill Gladstone and Ming Russell for reading my manuscript and giving me a shot. Bill Gladstone is a magnet for interesting people as well as someone who has literally run billions through the publishing houses in New York City. It was Bill's belief in this book that fueled its success.

Bill introduced me to Bill Simon, who is a master writer (particularly adept at organizational skills—something I have little patience for) with some *New York Times* bestsellers to his credit, and I am blessed to be working with someone who has such talent, experience, patience, humor and energy. We navigated a lot of emotional territory in the process of writing this book—mostly due to the challenges of Bill's personal life. I wish Arynne Simon a speedy recovery so that she can continue to enrich the lives of her friends, colleagues, family and our world.

From there, I want to thank Meredith, who offered me a book deal and was quite enthusiastic about the project, even when we selected to go with the veteran publisher, Roger Cooper, at Perseus Books. Meredith's first offer and her delightful encouragement gave us hope that we were really onto something (and a desirable backup plan in case Perseus didn't come through with an amazing deal).

Roger Cooper wowed me from the beginning with his complete understanding of the manuscript, as well as appreciating the deeper, more spiritual approach that I take with money. Under his aegis, this book had a real shot at staying true to the essence of what matters most to me—wealth interpreted to mean a life well lived and enjoyed, not just how many zeroes you manage to have in your bank account. Georgina Levitt was a delight to work with, and her suggestions were key to making this manuscript really sing. I've loved the entire team at Vanguard Press, including Francine LaSala, Jane Hilken, Amanda, Kay and the others who participated in making this book such a success.

My teenage son has been a dream while I've transitioned from caring for him (as Chief Everything Officer) to schlepping him everywhere (as the Chief ATM machine) to nurturing my life's passion (and becoming his head cheerleader). My family, including my dad, GK, Sammie, Denise, Christy, Davis, Peggy, Erwin, Laurel, Diane, Aunt Sue, Uncle Jerry, Wayne, Karen, Craig and Sean (and all of their spouses), have been so encouraging, even when I was in another city and missed key family events or was late to return phone calls and e-mails. I love you. Thanks for being there and for always encouraging me to let my wild side shine. (The interesting thing about losing your mother early is that you end up with even more family members, from all of the families who take you in. So, while I have missed my mother all of my life, I am also very thankful for the presence of the wonderful women who have stepped up to "mother" me in their own ways.)

There are more than thirty-five people who have provided professional services to help me launch, maintain and grow NataliePace.com, including the amazing WIN, Power of 10 Investment Club. Thank you Vicki, Linda, Patti, Joanie, Brigitte, Diane, Carol, Lulu and Lil for helping me to launch my dream-come-true life. I could not have done it without you, and I am forever indebted. Arlene Hylton-Campbell was so much fun to work with on the photo shoot. I hope we find more excuses to have me bathe in chocolate coins. I also couldn't have done it without the Mom Network—Marla, Harriet, Carmel, Marilyn and their delightful, entertaining and supportive husbands. Thanks to advisors and business colleagues, including Len Hartkemeier, Rene Fraser, Harriet Mouchley-Weiss, Brenda Zamzow, Douglas Simpson, Matt Walden, Reverend Joanne Coleman, Skip Rimer, Steve Forbes, Paul Maidment, Bruce Rogers, Dennis Kneale, Dave Andelman, Albert Bozzo, Dr. Rickie Byars Beckwith and Patty DeDominic.

Paul Woods and Meri-Ann Beck-Woods were the first to put their money into the business, and they have been regular contributors to the e-zine for years. Diane and George Mkitarian have been unbelievably loyal with their time, money and energy. Steve Martini, Patrick Fraoili, Jeffrey Glassman, Douglas Denoff, Sam Bartells, Sunil Rampersad, Kelley Wright, Peter Davidson and Greg Gimpel: quite simply, without their professional services (and outstanding creative minds), I couldn't have developed my ideas to the point of becoming an expert and writing this book. It was hilarious and heartwarming to have so many men in the bat cave when we were launching the Women's Investment Network, LLC. The wisdom and expertise of all of the early adopters in the Women's Investment Network, LLC and the first few thousand of my subscribers were key in the unfolding of this dream of spreading wealth by sharing wisdom, adding a splash of green to

Wall Street and transforming lives on Main Street. The gang over at the Infuzion Café in Santa Monica were my Theo in a time of need. I could not be here without any one of them.

Dr. Gary Becker and Michael Bernard Beckwith. These are two individuals whom I hold in the greatest esteem and awe. It's such a delight and an honor to have the author of "human capital" and the founder of Agape International Spiritual Center write the forewords to my book. These two men have contributed some of the most important ideas of humanity to the planet, and both have paved the path for an entire new way of thinking and living. They are my inspiration, my mentors and two people who inspire me to up my game.

However, there is one person, above everyone, who has been a constant, daily supporter, who has helped, inspired, guided and encouraged me to become a much more beautiful and well-rounded person, as a humanitarian, as a peacemaker, as a journalist, as a woman, as a budding economist, as a successful stock picker, as a mother and as a writer. Thank you, St. JJ. Without you, this book would not exist.

BILL SIMON

For an earlier book, I wrote this about my wife:

"I have this notion that there is a *right* person out there for everyone; it's just that some people aren't lucky enough ever to find their Mr. or Ms. Right. Others get lucky. I got lucky early enough in life to spend a good many years already (and count on spending many more) with one of God's treasures, my wife Arynne.

If I ever forget how lucky I am, I only need to pay attention to how many people seek and cherish her company. This is not the place to list her qualities; those who already know her have discovered the many for themselves, those who don't have a treat in store if they're ever fortunate enough to have the opportunity.

Let me just say that she puts up with the constant aggravation of living with a writer who has always worked at home but who gets grouchy about being disturbed when writing. There is a special place in heaven for such people. Arynne—I thank you for walking through life with me."

Today those sentiments are multiplied though under changed circumstances as I stand by Arynne's side offering support while she struggles to recover from a devastating illness. Yet she remains my inspiration and mainstay, my true love, as she will always.

As coauthors go, Natalie Pace is a dream. Smart, clever, fast, dedicated, witty and good company besides, she made this project a memorable journey from start to finish. So much so that I'm already looking forward to our next book together.

My tireless and loyal agent, Bill Gladstone, CEO of Waterside Communications, continues to delight me by coming up with projects on subjects so varied that I'm left in awe, and thoroughly delighted to be thrown into the path of so many fascinating people of such diverse interests and talents. This is the twenty-third book project that Bill has brought to me.

I'm blessed as well to have the support of the Waterside team, particularly my estimable backup agent Ming Russell, who watches my back, catches my slips and keeps track of the business side . . . and the always-reliable Maureen Malone, who has been a mainstay from my first book. Ever finding ways to make my life as a writer easier; Gladstone and his team are a joy to work with.

I've been blessed to work with some of the best publishers and editors in the business, and I'm delighted to be able to say I have now added Perseus and Roger Cooper to my personal list of "best in the business." Roger lived up to his reputation of being astute and insightful; those qualities, plus his way of always being available when I asked for guidance, made me a fan. Roger—many thanks.

Our editors Georgina Levitt and Francine LaSala offered structural suggestions that have strengthened the work to a degree I would not have anticipated and for which I offer a humble Bravo.

Finally, my thanks to copy editor Jane Hilken, who proved once again how much value a good copy editor brings to any book.

ABOUT THE AUTHORS

NATALIE WYNNE PACE

Natalie Pace has become the most trusted source of financial news, and her company, NataliePace.com, is one of the most widely read, independently owned and operated news organizations in the world. In 2006, Natalie Pace was the host of her own series of CEO Q&As on the Forbes.com Video Network. TipsTraders.com, an independent ranking agency that tracks over 830 A-list market gurus, has awarded her a number one ranking and named her a Highly Recommended Stock Picker in 2006 and 2007.

Natalie graduated summa cum laude from the University of Southern California with a degree in English literature, and she is a member of the Phi Beta Kappa and Phi Kappa Phi honor societies. She has helped to raise close to a million dollars for public schools in the Los Angeles area, and she is a founding member of the Los Angeles Donor's Circle, a group of 100 women dedicated to raising a million dollars to contribute to the financial literacy of women and girls in need.

Her favorite quote is: "We must be the change we wish to see," by Gandhi.

WILLIAM L. SIMON

Bill Simon is the author or coauthor of more than twenty-five books, including *New York Times* and international best sellers. He is also a screenwriter and a member of the Writers Guild of America, West. Though his undergraduate degree from Cornell University is in Electrical Engineering, his entire career has been spent as a freelance writer—originally writing television documentaries, informational films and corporate films. He holds a commercial pilot's license for fixed-wing aircraft and helicopters and has spent summers as a crewman on tallships. Bill lives in Los Angeles.